BOLIVIA

Robert Pateman

MARSHALL CAVENDISH
New York • London • Sydney

Reference edition published 1995 by
Marshall Cavendish Corporation
99 White Plains Road
P.O. Box 2001
Tarrytown
New York 10591

© Times Editions Pte Ltd 1995

Originated and designed by
Times Books International, an imprint of
Times Editions Pte Ltd

Printed in Singapore

Library of Congress Cataloging-in-Publication Data:
Pateman, Robert.
    Bolivia / Robert Pateman.
       p. cm.—(Cultures Of The World)
    Includes bibliographical references and index.
    Summary: Presents information on the history, geography,
religion, language, festivals, and other aspects of this land-
bound country of South America.
    ISBN 0-7614-0178-4 (lib. bdg.)
    1. Bolivia—Juvenile literature. [1. Bolivia] I. Title.
II. Series.
F3308.5.P37 1995
984—dc20   95–14899
                        CIP
                        AC

INTRODUCTION

THE REPUBLIC OF BOLIVIA is a land of snow-capped mountains and indigenous people with a rich and ancient culture.

Although the Altiplano—the high plain nestled in the Andes Mountains—forms the image most outsiders have of Bolivia, the country is a land of amazing contrasts. There are large areas of swamp, grassland, semi-desert, and tropical rainforest. Enormous mineral wealth lies hidden in the mountains, yet Bolivia remains one of the poorest countries in South America.

Two thousand of years of native civilization and 300 years of Spanish colonial rule have combined to produce the fascinating culture of modern Bolivia. Spanish festivals incorporate ancient Incan costumes. Ancient gods persist alongside the rituals of modern Catholicism. A rich heritage of dance, music, and weaving keeps old traditions alive.

CONTENTS

Native children on their way to school.

CONTENTS

Men do the knitting on Taquile Island in Lake Titicaca.

GEOGRAPHY

BOLIVIA IS NOT A LARGE COUNTRY compared with its South American neighbors, but it still covers 424,165 square miles (1,098,581 square kilometers), making it twice as big as Texas and only a little smaller than Alaska. It is a landlocked country with no direct access to the sea.

Bolivia shares borders with Peru and Chile to the west, Argentina to the south, Paraguay to the southeast, and Brazil to the east and north. Most of the population live on the High Plateau, or *Altiplano* ("ahl-tee-PLAH-noh"), between two chains of the Andes mountains. Most people would consider this region to be "typically Bolivian." However, the country also has large areas of tropical rainforest, savanna, swamp, and semidesert.

Bolivia has rich resources of minerals, and in the past much of the nation's wealth came from silver and tin mining. Today Bolivia has sufficient oil to meet its own needs.

Opposite: **The blue waters of Lake Titicaca are unusually clear and very deep.**

Left: **The spectacular cliffs of the Island of the Moon, one of the largest islands in Lake Titicaca.**

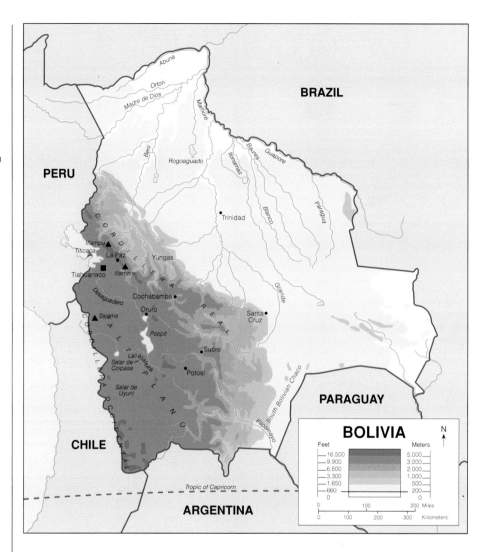

Despite its name, which means "swampy plain," Cochabamba is one of Bolivia's most beautiful cities, with a climate similar to Mediterranean Europe. It is surrounded by rich farmland, which has earned the region the title of "breadbasket of Bolivia."

THE DIFFERENT REGIONS

Bolivia has three main regions: the Altiplano or High Plateau, the Yungas, and the lowlands.

The Altiplano is one of the highest inhabited areas in the world. This plateau lies between two ranges of the Andes mountains at an average height of 12,000 feet (3,600 meters). It is a high, bleak, windswept, cold, and barren region. It is also the most densely populated region of Bolivia.

The Yungas are the deep valleys and high ridges on the eastern slopes

of the Andes. They are noted for their rugged terrain; hills and gorges tangle into each other, making many areas almost inaccessible. Although some valleys are narrow, others fan out into well-watered, fertile basins. This land is more fertile and more hospitable than the Altiplano, with a milder climate. Thirty percent of the population of Bolivia live in the valleys of the Yungas, which contain 40% of the country's cultivated land.

The lowlands, which lie to the north and east and stretch to Brazil and Paraguay, make up about three-fifths of Bolivia. The area around Trinidad is covered with rich tropical forests, part of the Amazon basin. Other areas are open savannas or swamps. In the south, the lowlands become the South Bolivian Chaco, part of the Gran Chaco. For nine months, this is a semidesert, but it turns into a swamp when the rains come. This is one of the hottest parts of South America during the rainy season, when temperatures of 100° F (37.8° C) are common. The Chaco is sparsely populated, as are the lowlands generally.

The Altiplano is about 80 miles (129 kilometers) across, and 500 miles (805 kilometers) long, spilling over into Argentina and Peru.

THE LEGEND OF ILLIMANI

Bolivian native culture has many wonderful legends. One tale concerns Mount Illimani. According to the legend, two mountains once stood above the place where the city of La Paz now stands. The god who created them could never decide which he loved the most. Both looked different in different light, and he was always walking across the canyon floor to see them at their best.

The god was watching Mount Illimani one day when he decided it really was his favorite. He hurled a giant boulder at the other peak, using his sling, and the second mountain top rolled far away. "Sajama," cried the god, which means go away. The mountain is still called by that name. The lower half of the mountain is still in its original place and is called Mururata, which means beheaded.

MOUNTAINS

The Andes mountains run the entire length of South America, from the northern coast to Tierra del Fuego at the southern end of Chile, a distance of 4,500 miles (7,241 kilometers). Before they enter Bolivia, the Andes divide into two ranges. The Cordillera Occidental runs through the west of the country and forms Bolivia's border with Chile. There are several active volcanoes in this range, and they occasionally give off gases. The highest point is Mount Sajama at 21,391 feet (6,519 meters).

The Cordillero Real passes to the east and reaches its most impressive point around La Paz, where there is a towering line of snow-capped peaks. The most famous of these is Mount Illimani at 21,200 feet (6,462 meters).

Farther south the Andes rejoin and widen. This forms the area known as the Puna. The Andes are rich in mineral deposits, including zinc, tin, and silver.

A mountainous land-scape. Four mountain peaks in western Bolivia rank among the highest in the world.

Due to its vast size and the bitter cold, the Uyuni Salt Flat has been called the Alaska of Bolivia.

RIVERS, SWAMPS, AND LAKES

Bolivia has three drainage systems: the Amazon system in the northeast, the Lake Titicaca system in the Altiplano, and a third that carries water southwest toward Argentina.

The Beni and Mamoré rivers collect much of the water that flows east from the Andes and form headwaters of the Amazon. Many rivers on the plains are deep enough to take shallow draft boats and barges and are important for transportation in an area where there are few roads. It is not possible to travel along the rivers to the Amazon proper and the sea beyond because of rapids.

A second drainage system starts on the Altiplano with hundreds of streams flowing down from the snowline into Lake Titicaca. The Desaguadero River flows south from Titicaca into Lake Poopó, a shallow, salty body of water rarely more than 10 feet (3 meters) deep. It usually covers 1,000 square miles (2,500 square kilometers), but after a heavy rain the lake can expand to the edge of Oruro, 30 miles (45 kilometers) away.

The Lacajahuira River flows south from Poopó and empties into the Coipasa Salt Field. This is a wide, marshy, salt-encrusted wilderness with one small body of water at the lowest point. The Uyuni Salt Flat lies farther south and is even bigger, covering 4,000 square miles (10,000 square kilometers).

The third drainage system is made up of water that runs off the Yungas and flows south into the Pilcomayo River and its tributaries. These run southeast to join the Paraguay River and the Plate.

CLIMATE

Because Bolivia is in the southern hemisphere, its summer and winter are the reverse of what they are in the northern hemisphere. Summer brings the most rain. Winter is generally drier and more pleasant, with day after day of clear blue skies. The higher areas get cold, and the temperature drops if the sun disappears behind a cloud for a few minutes. Between June and August, the fierce *surazo* ("soo-RAH-zoh") winds blow in from the Argentine pampas, bringing storms and severe drops in temperature.

The eastern slopes of the Andes below 6,000 feet (1,829 meters) are tropical. Average rainfall is 30–50 inches (76–127 centimeters) and neither temperature nor rainfall varies much.

The Yungas, from 6,000-9,500 feet (1,829–2,896 meters), are seldom cold. This area has the most pleasant climate, described as permanent spring. The Altiplano zone is always cool. Summer brings thunderstorms and winter occasional snow. Strong, cold winds blow across the plateau. Above 13,000 feet (3,962 m) there are arctic conditions.

In the rainforests, summer brings violent thunderstorms, which may cause rivers like this one to flood. In some years, this leads to major disasters that kill thousands of people.

Altitude has more influence on the climate of Bolivia than the seasons do.

13

Century plants grow at 13,000 feet (3,900 meters) and flower every 80 to 100 years.

FLORA AND FAUNA

Bolivia's vegetation is as varied as its climate. On the Altiplano, only hardy plants survive. Ichu, a coarse bunched grass, is the most common vegetation and is the basic food of the llama. Tola, a wind-resistant scrub, also grows here, as do cacti. Along the banks of Lake Titicaca, totora reeds are abundant. The Altiplano has no native trees, but eucalyptus has been introduced around the lake.

The Yungas have a wide range of natural trees, including cedar, mahogany, and walnut. One of the most useful is the cinchona, from which the malaria-fighting drug quinine was first extracted.

In the lowland plains, the flora varies with the rainfall. The Bolivian rainforest is a rich tropical forest with hundreds of species of trees, many of which grow to enormous heights. An equally diverse range of plants grows under the forest canopy.

The northern and central lowlands consist of grassy savannas and isolated woodlands, but farther south in the Chaco little survives the fierce conditions except cacti and scorched grasses.

Bolivia's wildlife is equally varied. In the highlands, the most striking animals are the llama, alpaca, guanaco, and vicuña, all native to the Andes and related to the camel. The llama and alpaca are domesticated versions of the guanaco. The vicuña is not kept domestically because it does not breed in captivity, but it is heavily hunted for its silky wool.

The Altiplano is also home to several species of rodents, including the cavy, a guinea pig bred for its meat and often kept as a pet. Predators include wolves and foxes.

Flora and Fauna

Lake Titicaca is home to many different species of birds, including gulls, ducks, geese, and hummingbirds. Lake Poopó to the south is famous for its flamingos, now endangered.

The Andes are also home to the Andean condor. This is a New World vulture and the largest flying bird in the Americas. It makes its nest at heights from 10,000 to 16,000 feet (3,048–4,877 meters) but descends to sea level on the western side of the Andes in search of food.

The swamps and plains of the lowlands have a very different ecosystem. Here are anteaters, a wild pig called a peccary, pumas, marsh deer, and the capybara, the world's largest rodent. The rivers and swamps are also home to countless numbers of fish, frogs, butterflies, toads, and lizards. The most remarkable bird of the region is the rhea, a large, flightless bird similar to an ostrich.

Many of these animals are hunted as food. The armadillo is considered a delicacy, and its shell can be used to make musical instruments. The only reason wildlife has survived so well is that the region has remained sparsely populated until now.

The semidesert area of the south brings another change in fauna. Animals that survive in these harsh conditions include anteaters, jaguars, and tapirs.

The most diverse wildlife of all is concentrated in Bolivia's tropical forests. Mammals include monkeys, anteaters, tapirs, jaguars, and the spectacled bear. The rivers are alive with fish, including the meat-eating piranha, and there are hundreds of species of birds and thousands of species of insects.

The Incas had a special respect for the puma. According to Bolivian folklore, when some of the moon disappears, it is because the puma has crept up and taken a bite out of it.

A baby mountain tapir and its mother. Tapirs eat plants, fallen fruit, and moss. They sleep during the day.

LAKE TITICACA

Lake Titicaca is remarkable because of its size, its altitude, and its great beauty. It is the second-largest lake in South America, covering 3,200 square miles (8,288 square kilometers), and has 36 islands. It is impossible to see the northwestern shore from the lakeside town of Copacabana. Its beauty comes from a combination of its deep color, the reflection of the blue sky, and in the south, the backdrop of mountain peaks.

In fact, Titicaca is almost two lakes; the smaller southern body of water is joined to the main lake only by a narrow strait. The border between Peru and Bolivia goes through the center of the lake, which means that traffic from La Paz has to cross the strait by ferry, rather than take the western shoreline route that would cross the Peruvian border. While buses and cars go across on small platforms, passengers transfer to little speedboats, which are tossed around by waves if there is any wind.

Titicaca lies at an altitude of 12,500 feet (3,810 meters) and is the highest navigable body of water in the world. It is also an exceptionally deep lake, reaching depths of about 900 feet (274 meters).

The lake played an important role in the religious beliefs of the early civilizations of the area. The Incas believed this was the spot where humankind was created. Rumors still persist that Lake Titicaca holds great hidden treasures. According to some accounts, the Incas threw vast amounts of gold and silver into the lake to prevent it being stolen by the Spanish. Other legends tell of ancient cities hidden beneath the deep waters of the lake.

ENDANGERED ENVIRONMENT

Bolivia's environment is facing new problems as roads are constructed to open up previously inaccessible areas, threatening Bolivia's wildlife. The government offers free land to families willing to move from the crowded Altiplano to the lowlands. Other sowers of environmental damage include the destruction of large sections of forest by timber companies and the poisoning of streams and rivers by gold prospectors, who use mercury to extract the gold.

Reserves and parks help preserve Bolivia's wildlife. The Reserve de Vida Salvaje Ríos Blanco Y Negro is the biggest, covering 3.4 million acres (1.4 million hectares) of rainforest.

THE DISPUTED CAPITALS

Sucre was the capital at Bolivia's independence and is still the judicial capital of Bolivia, but legislative and executive functions are located in La Paz. La Paz is the biggest city in Bolivia, with a population rapidly rising toward the one million mark. About half of the population is of native birth. La Paz was founded in October 1548 by Alonzo de Mendoza. The Spaniards hoped to find gold here but were disappointed. Instead, La Paz survived because of its position on the trade route between Potosí and Lima. It is the political, commercial, and industrial center of the nation.

Sucre lies southeast of La Paz. It has not grown as large as La Paz, but most people from Sucre believe their city is more beautiful, and it certainly has a milder, more pleasant climate. Founded in 1538, Sucre is still the most Spanish looking of Bolivia's cities, with many old colonial buildings.

At 11,900 feet (3,627 meters), La Paz is the highest city of its size in the world. The air is thin enough to cause some discomfort in breathing until one adjusts to the new conditions. La Paz sits in a canyon and is surrounded by snow-capped mountains, with four of the peaks rising higher than 20,000 feet (6,000 meters). The city has now outgrown the canyon, spreading out into neighboring valleys and onto the Altiplano.

HISTORY

THE HEARTLAND OF BOLIVIA consists of a vast area of arable land high up in the Andes Mountains on the great Altiplano, or High Plateau. The first people to inhabit this region were probably nomadic hunters who crossed the Bering Strait from Siberia and moved southward through the Americas.

By 1400 B.C., they were established on the great Altiplano, where they became farmers. Around this time, a new art style arose. Called Chavin, it was far more advanced than anything that had been produced previously.

Sometime between A.D. 500 and A.D. 800 there emerged an even more advanced culture, called Tiahuanaco, which was to influence people as far away as Ecuador. Farmers developed advanced methods of irrigation, and it was probably at this time that the potato was first cultivated.

The political and religious center of this civilization is believed to have been at Tiahuanaco, on the shores of Lake Titicaca, although there was an equally impressive sister city at Huari, in what is now Peru. The ruins at Tiahuanaco show that these people had developed the technology to transport enormous blocks of building stone across the lake. At its height, Tiahuanaco had a population of around 20,000 people, but after 300 or 400 years, it fell into decline. Nobody is sure why this happened. It might have been due to war, or perhaps the level of Lake Titicaca dropped, distancing the city from its vital water supply.

Above: **Carved faces on the wall of a temple at Tiahuanaco. The masonry at Tiahuanaco exhibits the earliest use of metal to hold stones together.**

Opposite: **The Columbus Monument in La Paz. In 1492 Christopher Columbus and his crew became the first Europeans since the Vikings to sail to the Americas.**

TIAHUANACO

The archeological site of Tiahuanaco lies about two hours' drive from La Paz. It is not, at first glance, a particularly impressive site because much of the stone has been carried away over the years to build churches and bridges.

There remain the mound of the Akapana, a great step pyramid, and the Kalasasaya (shown above), a great sunken temple. Just visible through the archway is the large sculpted figure that stands outside the Kalasasaya. Other sculptures include several freestanding statues, two carved doorways, and some stone faces in the walls of the sunken temple.

For archaeologists, Tiahuanaco is an exciting center that continues to produce surprises. Excavations in this century have revealed that the site was not just an isolated ceremonial center, as first thought, but a bustling metropolis that was home to thousands of people. Scientists have discovered evidence of a system of raised fields, which both protected the crops from the salty waters of Lake Titicaca and retained heat during the cold Altiplano nights.

The center of the pyramid has yet to be fully explored, and some archeologists hope to make a major find here that might rival the great treasures of the tomb of King Tutankhamen in Egypt.

THE INCAS

The decline of the Tiahuanaco empire left a power vacuum that was eventually filled by the dramatic rise of the Incan empire.

The Incas originally came from the Cuzco Valley in Peru, but from around A.D. 1400 they expanded to build an empire that stretched for 2,000 miles (3,000 kilometers) and probably had over four million subjects. To gain more control over the resistant Aymará people, the Incas moved many speakers of their language into the region.

An Incan wall still stands. From their capital in Cuzco, Peru, the Incas conquered a large territory and exported their technology and culture throughout the region.

The Incas were magnificent organizers and engineers. They constructed great cities linked by stone roads and established a system of runners to carry messages between cities. They built suspension bridges across wide gorges and terraced the mountainsides to grow crops. Incan artists worked in ceramics, silver, and gold. Their weavers produced magnificent textiles. These were so fine that the Spanish mistook Incan cotton for silk. Incan culture was rich in music and dance and had wonderful legends and folktales that were passed on by word of mouth. Many are still told today.

The Incas neither used the wheel nor developed a system of writing. The Incan empire left two major legacies: the ruins of their great cities and a language, Quechua, that is still spoken throughout much of South America. The Incan empire lasted little more than a hundred years before the Spanish swept them away. Whether Incan culture was already in decline by then is debatable, but they were certainly no match for the better-armed invaders who reached the borders of their empire in 1531.

An early engraving of Pizarro. Many of the Spaniards who came to Bolivia were searching for El Dorado, the legendary city so rich that the streets were paved in gold.

FRANCISCO PISARRO

ARRIVAL OF THE SPANISH

In 1492 Columbus became the first European since the Vikings to sail to the American continents. Pope Alexander VI decreed that this "pagan" land should be divided between Portugal and Spain. Inspired by the Pope's message, adventurers and soldiers set off to seek their fortunes in the new world.

Francisco Pizarro and Diego de Almagro were two Spanish adventurers who arrived at the Incan capital with just 170 soldiers. They found an empire facing serious political problems. The sudden death of the Lord Inca had left the leadership of the empire in doubt, and a civil war had broken out between two sons of the Inca, Huáscar and Atahualpa.

The Incan nobility were amazed by these strange, white-skinned, bearded men who rode on horses as if joined to the animal. As the Incas presumed that the *conquistadores* had been sent by the gods to settle the turmoil in the empire, the Spaniards met little resistance.

The Spaniards arranged a meeting with the victorious Atahualpa and imprisoned him. Although the Incas paid a huge ransom in gold and silver to get their leader back, the Spanish executed him and took over the empire.

Within two years, much of Incan society had been destroyed, and Pizarro and Almagro had divided South America between them. What is now Bolivia was ruled by Almagro and became known as Upper Peru or Charcas. Almagro's new wealth did him little good; he was assassinated by fellow Spaniards in 1538.

SILVER

In 1544, Diego Huallpa, a native herder, lost some llamas. Unable to find them, he made camp and lit a fire to keep warm. To his surprise, the earth beneath his fire started to flow in a stream of molten metal. Huallpa had discovered silver. This brought thousands of settlers to South America. By 1650 the town of Potosí had a population of 160,000 and was one of the greatest cities in the Americas. The silver mined at Potosí was taken to the coast on the backs of llamas. From there Spanish galleons ferried it across the Atlantic to Europe. For 200 years, the silver mines of Potosí (shown right) paid the Spanish empire's bills. According to local folklore, the Spanish took enough silver to build a bridge all the way to Spain.

The miners descended into the shafts by ropes, worked 12-hour shifts by candlelight, and were kept underground for days or weeks. Thousands died each year from disease, ill treatment, and accidents. Most of the work was done by natives brought in from all over the Andes. African slaves were imported, but few survived the cold. The mines were so feared that mothers deliberately crippled their sons so they would not be conscripted. It was at this time that the Spanish encouraged the miners to chew coca leaves to help them endure the wretched conditions. Previously, coca had been reserved for Incan priests and royalty.

La Paz was founded in 1548 as a staging point between the mines and the sea and soon became a major city. Oruro was the site of a second major silver find. Upper Peru was soon one of the wealthiest corners of the Spanish empire, and in 1559 a local government, the Audiencia of Charcas, was established under the control of the Viceroy of Peru. The government was based in Chuquisaca, which became the political and educational center of the colony.

Many of the Spanish who came to South America turned to farming and became the new landowning aristocracy. Because the Spaniards took the best land, the natives were pushed back to the higher mountain slopes, where they lived as tenant farmers, forced to supply the Spanish with food and labor.

SPAIN DECLINES

Plaza Murillo in La Paz was named after the rebel president, Pedro Murillo. Murillo was captured and executed on January 26, 1813.

The 1770s were a troubled time. After years of mistreatment, the indigenous population rebelled. The fighting lasted from 1770 to 1780. The rebels were finally captured and executed. Then there was an economic crisis. Between 1803 and 1825, silver production fell by 80%. By 1846, 10,000 mines had been abandoned.

In Upper Peru, unrest was growing among the Creoles (people of Spanish parents born in South America). Having played a major part in building Spain's American empire, they were angry that top government positions were reserved for those born in Spain.

Napoleon Bonaparte's conquest of Spain gave the colonies the perfect opportunity to rebel. In 1809, Creoles in Chuquisaca and La Paz declared that they would recognize the exiled Spanish king but not the governors sent by the French. On July 16, rebels in La Paz imprisoned the governor and elected Pedro Domingo Murillo president. The Spanish Viceroy in Lima sent an army and quickly crushed the revolution.

Some of the rebels fled to the hills and carried out a guerrilla campaign that lasted 16 years. Ironically, Upper Peru, which had started the revolution in South America, was the last colony to gain its freedom.

THE FIGHT FOR FREEDOM

Inspired by events in Upper Peru, revolution soon flared up across the continent. In 1814, Argentina won independence from Spain. In Europe, Napoleon was defeated and the Spanish monarchy restored, but South America had a taste for freedom, and the fight went on.

Simón Bolívar was a leading figure in this struggle. In a series of brilliant military campaigns, he brought independence to Venezuela, Colombia, and Ecuador. In 1824, he sent his revolutionary army to liberate Peru and bring colonial rule in South America to an end. Marshall Antonio José de Sucre was in charge of the campaign and won victories at Junín on August 6 and at Ayacucho on December 9 of the same year.

Historically, Upper Peru had always been linked with Lima, but that city had only just been freed from Spanish rule and there was no government in place. Many of the officers who had supported Sucre, particularly those who had deserted from the royalist army, wanted Upper Peru to be independent. Bolívar himself was against the idea and wanted the decision to wait until a new congress was formed in Lima. However, in February 1825, Sucre declared that Upper Peru must decide its own future, and on August 6, exactly a year after the first decisive battle, Upper Peru became an independent country, with Sucre as its first president.

Shortly afterward the new nation adopted the name Bolivia in honor of the great freedom fighter, and the city of Chuquisaca, where independence had been declared, became known as Sucre.

A monument to Antonio José de Sucre in La Paz. Sucre was called "the Immaculate" for his high moral qualities. He was assassinated in 1830 on his way home to Ecuador to retire.

BOLÍVAR—THE GREAT FREEDOM FIGHTER

Simón Bolívar was born in Caracas, Venezuela, in 1783. His father died when Bolívar was 3, and his mother six years later. As was usual for young men from upper-class South American families, he was sent to Spain to complete his education. He married the daughter of a Spanish nobleman and brought her back to South America. She died of yellow fever only a few months after arriving in her new home.

Bolívar visited Europe again in 1804, and it was then that he started to dream of an independent South America.

He returned to his homeland and joined the growing independence movement, which in 1810 expelled the Spanish governor from Caracas. Bolívar was sent to London, where he tried unsuccessfully to win British support for the struggle. He sailed back to South America, but when the revolution was crushed by troops loyal to Spain, he had to flee the country. While in exile, he wrote his most important political work, *El Manifiesto de Cartagena*, The Cartegena Manifesto.

In 1819, Bolívar marched his army across the snow-covered Andes and took the Spanish army by surprise. He won a series of brilliant military victories and became president of the newly independent nation of Gran Colombia. In 1824, his army, under the command of Antonio José de Sucre, crushed the last Spanish royalists in Ecuador and Peru.

Bolívar had the vision of uniting all of South America into one great nation and was disillusioned when the continent broke up into a collection of independent countries. He became unpopular as a leader and was nearly assassinated. He resigned as president and died in 1830, at the age of 47, worn out from a lifetime of fighting.

Bolívar himself might have been disappointed with the way events turned out, but to South Americans he will always be the legendary *El Libertador*.

DISASTROUS WARS

Although the individual South American nations had gained their independence, their borders were not clearly defined. As a result, Bolivia was dragged into a series of disastrous wars that resulted in the loss of large parts of its territory.

The first blow came 60 years after independence. Bolivia owned land on the coast that was rich with nitrates and guano (bird droppings used for fertilizer), but Bolivia was not in a position to exploit these resources. Instead, Bolivia gave Chile permission to develop them. A dispute developed over what taxes the Chileans should pay for this concession, and this led to war in 1879. Even though Peru came to Bolivia's aid, the Bolivian army was crushed at the Battle of Tacna. Bolivia played little part in the rest of the War of the Pacific and watched while Chile devastated Peru and took over a large part of Bolivian territory, including its access to the sea. Even today Bolivia's relationship with Chile is shadowed by the question of sea access.

The war discredited Bolivia's military leaders, and this allowed the rich mine owners to gain power. Around this time, mining started to recover from its earlier slump. The price of silver rose, and production increased as a result of investment in new equipment. In addition, industrialization in the West created a demand for tin, of which Bolivia had vast reserves.

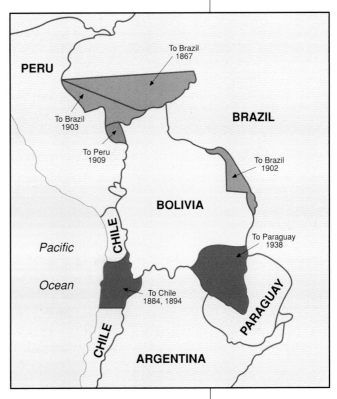

A series of wars with neighboring countries resulted in a large loss of land for Bolivia.

Veterans of the Chaco War. The war brought major changes to Bolivian society. Mestizos (people of mixed native and European ancestry) and Europeans had fought side by side, breaking down racial barriers and increasing the feeling of dissatisfaction among the people of mixed race. The war also inspired the Chaco Generation to change the way Bolivia was run. Some put their energy into art and literature, and others formed new political parties.

THE CHACO WAR

Bolivia had a liberal government from 1899 to 1920 and enjoyed one of the calmest periods in its history. World War I in Europe brought new demands for tin, but although demand was high, the price remained low.

In 1932, a border dispute with Paraguay developed. The two nations are separated by the Gran Chaco, a desert plain that no one had been concerned about. By the 1930s, there were rumors of oil in the region and the two nations started to argue over the position of the border. Bolivia set up a fort in the Chaco, which the Paraguayan army seized. Negotiations were taking place when the troops on the ground started fighting. The conflict escalated rapidly. Two oil companies, hoping to win rights to develop whatever oil was found, provided funds to cover the cost of the war. Having just lost a war, Paraguay saw this as an opportunity to restore national pride.

The war lasted three years and ended in defeat for Bolivia. As many as 100,000 Bolivians were either killed, wounded, or captured. At the end,

Bolivia had lost another large part of her territory. Ironically, no oil was ever discovered in the disputed territory.

MODERN HISTORY

The years following the Chaco War were a period of strikes and military coups. Several new political parties were formed, the most important of which was the *Movimiento Nacionalista Revolucionario* (MNR). The MNR drew support from mine workers and peasants to win the 1951 election. However, before the MNR could take power, the army staged a coup. The army met with fierce resistance from the miners, who triumphed in the April Revolution of 1952 and placed the MNR in power.

Victor Paz Estenssoro became president and introduced a far-reaching range of reforms. Mines were nationalized, the native population was given the right to vote, land laws were reformed, and primary education was introduced into the villages. The MNR remained in power for 12 years. However, the MNR failed to improve the standard of living for the general population and so lost popularity. In 1964, there was a military coup.

This proved to be the start of another period of instability, with one military government replacing another. At the worst times, particularly during the late 1970s, presidents resorted to imprisoning and torturing people, and many of their opponents simply "disappeared." Probably the worst of the dictators was General Luis García Meza.

In 1985, Victor Paz Estenssoro became president for the third time. He introduced some harsh economic reforms but managed to make both the political situation and the economy far more stable. There are still major issues to be faced, including opening up the economy and controlling the growing of coca. However, today many Bolivians are cautiously optimistic about their country's future.

In 1967, the Marxist hero Che Guevara, who had been training guerrillas in southern Bolivia, was captured and killed by the Bolivian army.

GOVERNMENT

BOLIVIA IS A REPUBLIC with the president as head of state. Presidents are elected for four-year terms and select a cabinet of ministers to help them run the country. Presidents have the right to rule by decree.

At election time, presidential candidates nominate a running mate and they campaign together. Elections are highly charged affairs, with aggressive campaigning. The national television station gives all candidates equal air time, but parties can buy additional time on other stations. Generally people have been cynical about elections, unsure what might happen or how fair they will be. However, as the country prepares for its third election without military interference, there is growing public confidence in the new political maturity.

If there is no clear majority, parliament has final say. This means weeks of bargaining behind closed doors. In 1989, Gonzalo Sánchez de Lozada won the most votes but did not have enough support to form a majority. The second-place candidate, General Hugo Bánzer Suárez, gave his support to Jaime Paz Zamora, who had finished third. This surprised most people because the two men had been adversaries.

Once a president is in office, the power the president wields is often determined by personal authority and popularity. Strong presidents often rule without answering to parliament or any other authority.

In the past, the military has often removed governments by force. Strikes by labor unions have also disrupted the country. Another problem is the vast army of bureaucrats, which makes governing a slow and frustrating experience.

Above: Every village in Bolivia has a memorial to the Chaco War, in which 10,000 Bolivians lost their lives. The Chaco War was as traumatic to Bolivia as the Vietnamese War was to the United States, and caused the whole nation to lose faith in itself.

Opposite: A military parade in La Paz. The military has played a large role in Bolivian politics.

Government offices in La Paz.

CONGRESS

The congress, or *Congreso Nacional,* consists of two houses: a chamber of deputies and a senate. Congresss generally meets for a 90-day session.

Each of the country's departments has an allocation of seats in congress according to its population. Until 1952, only literate people could vote. This was one method the aristocracy used to retain power. Since 1952, all married Bolivians over 18 and all single people over 21 have the right to vote. Now the vote is to be extended to everyone over 18.

The chamber of deputies consists of 130 members elected for four-year terms. The senate is made up of 27 senators—three from each department—and 130 deputies. Members of congress are elected by popular vote and serve a six-year term. The vice president is the presiding officer of the senate. The role of the senate is to review and approve the work of the chamber of deputies.

The third branch of authority is the judiciary. The supreme court is based in Sucre and consists of 13 judges selected by congress. Judges serve 10-year terms on the supreme court.

This system of government is similar to that in the United States. Bolivia, like the United States, has a constitution that lays down basic freedoms and rules for government. However, the Bolivian constitution has often been ignored or suspended by politicians, and the military often overrides the constitutional process.

THE AYNI SYSTEM

On the Altiplano, most decisions are still made at village level by the *ayni* ("AYE-nee"), a political, economic, and social system that has been in place at least since Incan times. Under the ayni system, the men of the village meet to discuss what needs to be done. Once a decision is made, everyone works together on the project for the good of the community.

The *jilakata* ("HEE-lah-kah-ta"), or chief, has a particularly important role to play. After listening to discussion, he makes the final decision. Generally the chief is selected by age, but factors such as personality and community support are also important. Acts of god also help. The Altiplano often has lightning storms, and anyone who survives being hit by lightning wins awe and prestige.

The anyi system also works in a less formal way. At a wedding, all the villagers bring gifts, perhaps sheep or beer. This helps the family afford the expensive celebration. However, the ayni system demands that you give back twice as much as you received. If someone brought four sheep to your son's wedding, you have to give eight back when there is a wedding in their family.

At election time, the modern political system meets the ayni system. Elections, at least since 1985, have been freely conducted in Bolivia, and every villager gets a chance to vote. However, in the weeks before the polling station arrives, the village usually holds an ayni meeting at which it is decided how everyone is going to vote.

LOCAL GOVERNMENT

Bolivia is divided into nine departments, each ruled by a prefect appointed by the president. The departments are subdivided into provinces, which are controlled by subprefects, also selected by the president. Subprovinces are divided into cantons. Important cities have their own elected council led by an elected mayor.

Although local governments do much of the administration, important decisions are usually made by the central government. In addition, by keeping control over many key appointments, the president can impose authority over the whole system. As presidents do not appoint people who are likely to oppose them, politicians who want to further their careers know they can do so only with the president's support.

At present, there is a major campaign to convince people that a new Bolivia can be built on participation and education reform. Bolivians, however, being used to numerous such campaigns, remain cynical about the government's ability to put its good intentions into practice.

One of the major promises of the current government is to decentralize government and give more power to local politicians.

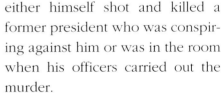

POLITICS BY FORCE

Bolivian politics have often been violent and unpredictable, with few presidents finishing a full term. On many occasions, the army has nullified elections and seized power. In 1980, the country recorded its 189th coup in 155 years of independence.

As a result, Bolivia has had some brazen and ruthless heads of state, many of whom became increasingly authoritarian and dictatorial while in office, ignoring the constitution and suppressing human rights.

One of the worst was President Mariano Melgarejo, who was in power from 1865 to 1871. During his years in office, he diverted vast amounts of the nation's wealth into his own pockets. He seized land from the native people and conceded large areas of northern Bolivia to Brazil. In an incident that is still shrouded in mystery, it is suspected that Melgarejo either himself shot and killed a former president who was conspiring against him or was in the room when his officers carried out the murder.

Bolivia has also produced some highly respected presidents, including Antonio José de Sucre, founder of the country and its first president; Andrés de Santa Cruz, a powerful and influential figure known as the Napoleon of the Andes; and Ismael Montes, who served two terms in office, from 1904 to 1909 and from 1913 to 1917. Montes was one of the

General Luis García Meza came to power in a 1980 military coup. For 14 months, he suppressed all opposition by imprisoning, torturing, and murdering opponents. When Meza was finally ousted, the Bolivian economy was deep in debt.

In April 1994, Meza was tried for his crimes by the supreme court and sentenced to 30 years in jail. At present, however, Meza is in exile in Brazil and looks unlikely to return to Bolivia. Many of the people who took part in his government are serving prison sentences.

first politicians to be concerned about the rights of the native community.

Victor Paz Estenssoro, leader of the MNR, served several terms in power. He implemented many reforms after the 1952 revolution and proved himself willing to make unpopular decisions to correct a troubled economy.

At the moment, the Bolivian government is enjoying a remarkably stable period, and has hopefully entered an era of new political maturity. In August 1989, Jaime Paz Zamora completed a full term of civilian rule and then presided over a peaceful handover. It was the first time in 20 years that the presidency changed hands through the democratic process.

The current president is Gonzalo Sánchez de Lozada, known to everyone as "Gondi." As minister of planning, he was given much of the credit for the economic reform of the 1980s. Bolivians seem to like his policies more than the man himself. Perhaps one of the problems is that he spent much of his life out of the country, and people joke that he speaks Spanish like a *gringo.*

Gonzalo Sánchez de Lozada is the current president of Bolivia.

Only one Bolivian woman has ever served as president. Lidia Gueiler Tejada was interim president from November 1979 to July 1980.

Victor Paz Estenssoro in 1985. His 1952 government assumed control over the tin mines and granted the native peoples full civil rights.

THE 1952 REVOLUTION

The revolution of 1952 was the single most dramatic event in Bolivian politics. It started a chain of events that still affects the country.

By the 1950s, most Bolivians were unhappy about conditions in their country; the majority of people were living in poverty, while a small elite enjoyed most of the wealth and political power.

The newly formed MNR promised to reform this situation and won widespread support among the peasants and miners.

Under the skillful leadership of Victor Paz Estenssoro, the MNR won the 1951 election, only to have power snatched away from it by a military coup. On this occasion, however, the mood in the nation was different. A popular revolution broke out and after several pitched battles, each one more violent, the army was crushed and Estenssoro's civilian government was placed in power.

The revolutionary government immediately nationalized the mines and started a series of economic and educational projects. Most importantly, in August 1953 the government implemented one of the most far-reaching land reform acts of the century, giving native farmers ownership of any land they farmed. The new government also broke the absolute power of the small ruling elite by giving every adult Bolivian citizen the right to vote. Previously, the franchise had been extended only to the literate.

FLAG AND EMBLEM

The Bolivian flag is divided into three horizontal stripes of red, gold, and green. The flag was first used by the president in 1851 and was adopted as the nation's flag in 1888. The red in the flag represents both animals and the armed forces, the green is for fertility and the land, and the yellow is for the nation's mineral wealth.

The national emblem (shown here) includes a condor, Mount Potosí, and a woolly alpaca.

The Bolivian national anthem is the *National Hymn of Bolivia*.

FOREIGN POLICY

The search for access to the sea dominates Bolivian foreign policy. Every time a political party starts to become unpopular, it brings up this issue. There seems no possibility of Chile conceding land to Bolivia, and the issue looks likely to remain a thorn between the nations for years to come.

Bolivia also faces occasional border conflicts with Brazil. These may increase as both start to develop the wilderness areas that lie along the border. Bolivia has the best relationship with Argentina, a major trading partner, and many Bolivians work there. In 1992, Bolivia developed closer trading ties with its neighbors by officially joining the Andean Free-Trade Area, which removes trade barriers between members. There is also talk of Bolivia being the first South American nation to join the North American Free-Trade Agreement (NAFTA).

Bolivia follows the international lead of the United States, from which it receives considerable financial aid. The United States supports Bolivia in hopes of strengthening democratic government and pressuring the government to curtail the illegal cultivation and export of coca. However, when U.S. troops were used for antidrug raids, it was a blow to Bolivian autonomy, and there were protests outside the U.S. embassy.

In January 1992, Bolivia signed an agreement with Peru that granted Bolivia free sea access from the border town of Desaguadero to the Pacific port of Ilo, Peru, until 2091.

ECONOMY

DESPITE ITS MINERAL WEALTH, Bolivia is one of the poorest countries in South America and relies on foreign aid, especially from the United States. Bolivia's Gross National Product (GNP) is $680 per person, compared with $3,100 in Argentina, and over $22,000 in the United States. Many Bolivians live below the poverty line.

There are various reasons why the country remains so poor, including the rugged landscape, which makes transportation and development difficult, and the lack of a direct access to the sea.

Government polices have not always helped, and foreign companies that might have invested have been discouraged by the country's political instability. Even though the present government is more open to outside investment, there are bureaucratic obstacles that discourage foreign companies. The government is pushing ahead with a program of capitalization, which President Gonzalo Sánchez de Lozada has said will "change Bolivia forever." Many Bolivians believe that the new era of political stability will be accompanied by economic growth. There is a great deal of optimism about the nation's ability to develop the vast resources of the tropical lowlands.

Opposite: **Harvesting quinoa. Farming, which employs nearly half the population, is hampered by the poor soils of the Altiplano. Agriculture makes relatively little contribution to exports, and Bolivia must import food.**

INFLATION ALERT

At one point inflation in Bolivia was running at 24,000 percent per year. In other words, every item in Bolivia cost 240 times its original price by the end of the year. That means that a candy bar that cost 50 cents on January 1 would cost $120 by December 31!

Under these circumstances, nobody wanted to keep their money in the bank, so they either spent it at once or converted it to U.S. dollars. At the height of the inflationary period, it cost 1.4 million bolivianos to buy one U.S. dollar.

Once inflation was under control, the government issued new bank notes. One million old bolivianos were exchanged for one new boliviano.

Mining remains a dangerous occupation. In December 1993, a landslide in the Llipi gold fields killed over 200 people.

Mines, like this tin mine, are common sights all over Bolivia. Tin used to be Bolivia's top export, but has recently been replaced by gas. Other minerals in Bolivia are tungsten, antimony, zinc, gold, and silver.

MINERAL WEALTH

Virtually every valuable mineral is found in Bolivia. Bolivia is the world's largest producer of bismuth and the second-largest producer of antimony. Gold and silver are also exported. Tin used to be the most important export. The fall in tin prices in the mid-1980s was devastating for Bolivia, whose tin is expensive to extract. For every $2.50 the country received for tin, it spent $10 to mine and transport it. Many mines were closed and unemployment soared, as 28,000 miners lost their jobs.

Mining accounts for 11% of the GNP and employs about 9% of the work force. The *Corporación Mineral de Bolivia* runs the larger mines and leases others to miners' cooperatives.

Bolivia's oil fields produce from 25,000 to 30,000 barrels a day, and domestic consumption is about 25,000 barrels a day, so there is occasionally a surplus for export. The oil fields were first developed in the 1920s by Standard Oil Company of Bolivia, a U.S.-based company. The government took over the fields in 1937. Only after the 1952 revolution did the industry start to receive the investment capital it required.

Recently, the natural gas fields have given a boost to the economy. Bolivia uses very little natural gas; most is sold to Argentina and Brazil. A gas pipeline runs into Argentina, and there are plans to open a pipeline to Brazil by 1996. Gas has replaced tin as the top export commodity and accounts for about 36% of the country's total official exports.

With its many mountains and rivers, Bolivia has considerable potential for producing hydroelectric power. The first projects have been built in the vicinity of La Paz and Cochabamba.

AGRICULTURE

Agriculture employs about 50% of Bolivians, yet Bolivia cannot grow sufficient food to feed its population. Farming is held back by antiquated methods. On the Altiplano much of the work is still done by hand, and the poor soil barely provides sufficient food for each family to survive. The government is trying to introduce new methods, but many of the native peoples in this region do not accept changes easily.

The more fertile Yungas produce much of the food for La Paz and other cities. These warmer, more fertile areas grow a wider range of fruit and vegetables, including bananas, oranges, turnips, carrots, and cassava, as well as export-quality coffee. The Santa Cruz and EL Beni departments have over four million head of cattle. The beef is largely for the domestic market, with some exported to Peru and Brazil.

Traditionally the rainforest has added little to the economy, except brazil nuts and latex. There is great potential for extracting tropical hard woods, causing growing conflict between economists and environmentalists.

Many hillsides are terraced in order to increase arable land. Terraced hillsides in Bolivia go back to the time of the Incas.

Bolivia makes many of the products required by the domestic construction industry, and there are brickyards and cement factories. However, the country has no facilities for heavy industry and has to import motor vehicles and most electrical and consumer goods.

INDUSTRY

Because of the small population and the limited spending power of most of the people, Bolivia has only a small market for manufactured goods.

Much of Bolivian industry is still based in small or medium-sized factories, which produce items to meet daily needs, including textiles, shoes, and blankets. Two-thirds of factories in Bolivia are based in or around La Paz. Santa Cruz and Cochabamba are the other major industrial centers.

Larger factories have been set up to support the mining industry. There are also several oil refineries. Other factories use byproducts from oil to produce a wide range of items.

Another important industrial sector is linked with food processing, particularly sugar, coffee, and rice. There is hope that Bolivian grains, such as quinoa, can be promoted in the United States and Europe as health foods. Several cities have large breweries, and local wine is also made in the south of the country.

Industry officially employs about 10 percent of the work force, but a great deal of manufacturing takes place in small, family-run workshops employing only two or three people. Such places are seldom registered and operate outside the official figures.

In recent years, many new industrial projects have begun operations. These range from a ceramic tile industry in Sucre to a new textile factory in Tarija that combines angora wool with cotton.

WORK ETHIC

Generally Bolivians are hard workers who take pride in what they do. However, the country lacks skilled workers, and setting up new projects often involves a considerable amount of basic training. Unfortunately, people who work with their hands are looked down on, while doctors, lawyers, and architects, for example, are admired.

Bolivian workers sometimes lack discipline. It is not unusual for people to take a two- or three-hour lunch break, or simply not turn up for work. This situation is particularly true in government offices, which can make it extremely frustrating for people trying to complete important paper-work.

People in government employment are often poorly paid, and it is not unusual for them to have second or third jobs. Government employees often supplement their incomes with bribes.

Bolivian workers can be militant and often try to get issues changed by force, particularly by striking. Riot police have been called in to break up protests. This reaction runs all through Bolivian society. A maid wanting an increase in pay is likely to quit, then negotiate a higher wage to stay on.

Some of the hardest workers are the indigenous women. In addition to domestic chores, they put in long hours on the land or on street corners selling goods. The income they bring in makes a major contribution to the family.

An estimated 10% of the population is unemployed, and considerably more are underemployed, doing jobs that do not pay enough to support a family.

Street workers in La Paz.

Intercity buses are often overcrowded, with people standing, luggage piled up on the roof, and chickens pushed under the seats. In cities buses are supplemented by private minibuses and *trufi* ("TROO-fee"), cars which drive along set routes, picking up passengers as they go. Trufi charge a fraction more than the bus, and can be identified by the two flags they fly on the hood.

TRANSPORTATION

Bolivia moved from transport by animals to transport by airplane without developing the stages in between. Although the road system covers 25,000 miles (40,000 kilometers), little of it is paved. In a country where there is one car per 150 people, everyone makes the best of what is available. Hitchhiking is common, and trucks take passengers on the return journey.

There are 2,260 miles (3,630 kilometers) of railway line, including a vital link with Antofagasta in Chile, but the system is badly organized. Trains are slow and often delayed. In addition, the eastern and western systems do not join up. It has been left to the state-owned airline to fill in the gaps.

In the lowlands, Bolivia's navigable rivers offer considerable potential. There is even talk of a major project, the Hydrovia, a river highway that will pass through five countries and link Puerto Suarez in Bolivia to the Rio de la Plate. The Hydrovia is still in the planning stage, and if the project does get under way, it will involve dredging and building embankments and might cost as much as $2 billion.

COCA

Coca, used to make the drug cocaine, is widely believed to be the top Bolivian export. At one point, the coca trade was thought to earn Bolivia about $600 million a year. But this figure is only a guess because international trade in coca is illegal.

Bolivians have been chewing coca and drinking it in tea for centuries. This is legal and an accepted part of the culture. The Pope and Queen Sofia of Spain have tried coca tea. Bolivia makes many coca products, including wine, soap, face cream, medicine, chewing gum, and toothpaste. Whatever the merits of coca itself, when made into cocaine, it becomes dangerous and is illegal.

Most Bolivian coca grows in the Yungas and the Chapare region of North Cochabamba. Coca from the Yungas is used domestically, but the Chapare crop is shipped to laboratories hidden deep in the rainforest, where it is turned into cocaine. This is sent to Colombia, the center of international cocaine-trafficking rings. From there it is smuggled into the United States and Europe.

Many politicians have been suspected of being involved in the drug trade, but recent administrations have attempted to limit the cultivation of coca. Reports suggest that strategies such as paying farmers to destroy their crop have reduced the amount of Bolivian coca reaching the international market. However, many coca growers are unemployed miners who do not have the knowledge to switch to other types of farming.

BOLIVIANS

THE POPULATION OF BOLIVIA has now passed the seven million mark, not a large number for a country so vast. There are fewer people in Bolivia than in Ohio or Florida. However, the population is not evenly distributed. The lowland plains are underpopulated, and 70% of all Bolivians live on the Altiplano. Only about half the population live in cities, a low percentage for a Latin American country.

The Bolivian population is made up of three main groups: natives, *mestizos*—those with mixed Spanish and native blood—and those who claim to be direct descendants of the Spanish. About 60% of the population belong to the two largest native groups, the Quechua and the Aymará.

The lowland people tend to reflect the warm sunny weather of their region. They wear brighter colors and lighter clothes and have the reputation of being the liveliest dancers. Generally thought of as being more adventurous, they tend to ignore minor rules and regulations. Part of the reason the lowland economy is booming is that people there are willing to take more chances.

Highlanders tend to be more conservative and restrained. People from La Paz, in contrast, are more conservative in their dress and their behavior. They believe they give the country the stability it needs and that they hold back some of their fellow citizens' rasher instincts.

Above: **A native child in La Paz. Native people constitute the bulk of the lower classes.**

Opposite: **A native woman spins wool in Ayacucha.**

THE HIGHLAND NATIVES

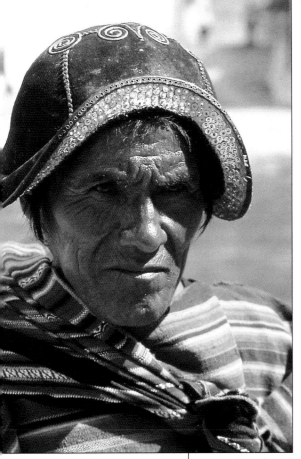

Highland natives are a rugged, strong-spirited people who have retained much of their culture and identity. The two main groups are the Aymará and the Quechua.

Both groups have slightly larger lungs than average to take in more oxygen and extra blood vessels in their limbs to help keep them warm. The Quechua mainly live in the south of the Altiplano, around Cochabamba and Sucre. The Aymará farm the land around La Paz and Lake Titicaca. The two seldom mix, and intermarriage is rare.

Many from both groups have left the countryside to seek work in cities. Initially the breaking of family ties led to problems with alcohol abuse. People have since adjusted, and the second and third generations, with the advantage of education, have become quite prosperous.

Although native labor was always important to the economy, indigenous people remain isolated from mainstream life. It is only since the 1952 revolution that there have been attempts to change this, and only in 1975 that Quechua and Aymará were made official languages.

THE QUECHUA The Quechua are spread across Peru, Bolivia, and Ecuador. Traditionally they lived in isolated agricultural communities. Recently, many have moved to cities to find employment, particularly in construction. The urban communities are likely to be bilingual and their lifestyle less traditional.

In rural communities, home is a small, one-room building made of sun-dried bricks and a thatched roof. A hearth stands in one corner for the fire.

The main crop is potatoes, and their livestock usually includes llamas. These are rarely slaughtered but are occasionally sold when money is needed. The wool is made into shawls and ponchos, which the women weave on a traditional peg loom. The family might also keep an alpaca, but its wool is more likely to be sold than used for the family.

Looking after the animals is usually the job of the youngest children, who are put to work as soon as they can walk. After the age of 11 or 12, the task of looking after livestock is passed on to younger siblings, and the older children start to help their parents in the fields.

THE AYMARÁ The Aymará probably arrived at Lake Titicaca sometime between 1400 and 400 B.C. It is likely that they came from central Peru, although their arrival in this region is an unsolved historical mystery. They were a fiercely independent people and were able to retain their language after being conquered by the Incas.

The Aymará resist change, and life in rural areas is similar to what it must have been like 1,000 years ago. A typical rural home is built from mud bricks and is either a one-room building or a two-story house. There are likely to be some outbuildings, and the whole complex might be surrounded by a mud-brick wall. A few roofs are still thatched, but corrugated metal is now widely used. Cooking and washing are done outside.

The Aymará grow barley, potatoes, beans, onions, and garlic. In the warmer valleys, they might even be able to produce corn and fruit. Many supplement their diet, or earn a living, from fishing.

A Quechua man *(opposite)* and a young Aymará girl *(below)*. The Aymará are a single group united by language and a common culture. The Quechua consist of many groups who share the same language but consider themselves culturally distinct. Both the Quechua and Aymará are typically short, with broad faces, dark skin, and black hair.

THE KALLAWAYA The Kallawaya come from the eastern shore of Lake Titicaca. They are probably related to the Aymará, although their origins are unknown. Legend claims they are direct descendants of the Tiahuanaco.

The Kallawaya are farmers and healers. They are knowledgeable about the healing properties of herbs, using various plants to effect their cures. The Kallawaya also use spells, charms, and amulets to aid in a cure.

The Kallawaya ability to cure is respected throughout Bolivia and Kallawaya healers can be found all over the country. Several foreign scientists are now studying Kallawaya methods. For the Kallawaya, sickness and disease occur when there is an imbalance of *ajallu* ("ah-HAH-yu"), or life force.

Because of their nomadic lifestyle, Kallawaya men tend to be multilingual, able to speak various native dialects as well as Spanish. In addition they have their own "secret" language. A legend claims that because of their healing skills, the Kallawaya were taken to the Incan capital and still speak the language of the ancient royal court.

THE CHIPAYA The Chipaya live in one of the most remote parts of the Altiplano, around Coipasa Salt Field. Nobody is sure why they moved to such an inhospitable area, but they probably sought refuge there from the more aggressive Aymará. They now number about 1,000 and are more or less restricted to one village.

Kallawaya people are recognized by the woven headbands that are worn by the women and the medicine pouches of the men. Their weaving is also distinct and colorful. The women wear striped shawls, the colors of which identify the region they are from.

The Chipaya look similar to the Aymará but generally have broader faces and darker skin. They tend to wear rough-looking cloth of beige, brown, and black. Chipaya women are easily distinguished by the way they braid their hair into hundreds of small plaits.

The Chipaya survive by farming and keep llamas and sheep. Unlike the Aymará, hunting plays an important part in their lives. Another distinctive feature is the architecture of their huts, which are round. The Chipaya surround their village with mud-built, whitewashed cones, in which offerings are placed to keep evil spirits away.

The Chipaya have accepted some ideas from the outside world, particularly in dress. The men now wear the tight-fitting woolen hats of the Aymará to protect themselves from the cold. They have started to wear simple rubber shoes cut from old car tires.

The Roman Catholic religion has arrived in the Chipaya village but has not replaced traditional beliefs.

Chipaya creep out into the lake in search of ducks and geese. Their weapon is the *bolas*, a Y-shaped cord with lead weights on each end. A skillful hunter can bring a bird down in midflight. The Chipaya also leave string traps across streams to catch birds as they take to the air. Unfortunately they often catch rare flamingoes, whose feathers are used as hat ornaments.

The last member of the Uru, a people similar to the Chipaya, died just after World War II.

A group of Guaraní people. In 1990, 500 lowland natives made a dramatic protest march to La Paz, seeking government protection for their jungle home. They demanded acknowledgment that 4 million acres (1.6 million hectares) of forest belonged to them, new laws to protect them and their forest, and a deadline for logging companies to leave the Chimanes forest.

THE LOWLAND NATIVES

In isolated regions of the lowland plains, particularly in the tropical forests, there are still tribes living a traditional lifestyle, almost unaware of the outside world. The Guaraní, Guarayo, and Chiquitano each number between 15,000 and 20,000 people, but all the other tribes total only 15,000 altogether.

Generally lowland natives have little in common with the rest of Bolivia. They do not speak the same language, share the same culture, or even look the same. In appearance, lowland natives tend to be short, dark-skinned people with Negroid hair.

Their lifestyle is very simple. They might practice some slash-and-burn farming but generally survive on what the jungle provides for them. Technology is limited to a few simple tools and weapons. Houses are usually temporary constructions and some of the smaller groups, such as the Yaqui, do not build homes at all. A few groups have apparently lost the knowledge of making fire.

THE SIRIONO

The Siriono, who are part of the Guaraní group of people, live in the tropical forests of Bolivia. Like most of the forest peoples, they are short; even the men seldom grow taller than 5'4".

Even as recently as 30 years ago the Siriono lived a semi-aboriginal existence. The men were skillful hunters, catching armadillos, monkeys, and tortoises. They also caught fish with a bow and arrow.

Both men and women gathered fruit and other food from the surrounding rainforest, but other work was strictly segregated between men and women. House building and tree chopping was men's work. Weaving, caring for the children, cooking, and twining hammocks was considered women's work.

The Siriono apparently had no knowledge of making fire. Anthropologists who stayed in Siriono society watched them carefully protect glowing embers whenever the village moved site, but they were never seen to start a new fire.

Siriono art mainly consisted of elaborate body painting. They also had their own music and dances, and with the sunrise the whole village would wake and start singing. Dancing was an evening activity. However, the Siriono would never dance on moonless nights.

Today there are about 1,500 Sirioni surviving in several different areas. In 1992 the government put aside a reserve for them. However in many ways their isolation has been broken. Agriculture plays an increasing role in their lives, and it is not uncommon to see the men wearing western clothing.

In towns people often use the word chola *("CHOH-lah") to refer to native women who wear traditional dress. It is acceptable to say to a third person, "Look at those cholas over there," but rude to call an individual a chola to their face.* Cholita *("choh-LEE-tah") carries more affection and is sometimes used to address a person one is familiar with.*

Generally, the tribes that lived along the rivers enjoyed the most favorable environment and developed the more advanced cultures. It was also these people who had the first contact with the Europeans, and therefore their culture has undergone the most drastic change. Many groups have abandoned their old way of life and found work in the river settlements or rubber plantations.

Now even the most remote tribes, which had previously managed to retain their isolated lifestyle, are finding themselves threatened as new roads are cut through the forest.

THE SPANISH

A significant number of people in Bolivia still claim to be directly descended from the early Spanish colonists. Locally they are known as *blancos* ("BLAN-kohs"), meaning whites, *la gente decente* ("la HAIN-tay day-SAIN-tay"), meaning the decent people, or *la gente buena* ("la HAIN-tay BWAY-nah"), meaning the good people.

A little boy with distinctive Spanish coloring is dressed up for his baptism.

It is difficult to know how many people fall into this category, especially because there has been much intermingling of the races. After four centuries, many of those who claim to be from 100% Spanish stock could probably find native or other blood somewhere in their family history if they researched back far enough.

Yet in the past, this group was remarkably homogeneous and fiercely protective of their Spanish heritage. As a result, there is a distinct group who are light skinned and indistinguishable in appearance from people who have never left Spain.

The old-fashioned concept of being Spanish is made up of a combination of factors, of which purity of blood is just one. Other characteristics of being Spanish include a sense of aristocracy, a code of moral behavior, a high level of education, fluency in Spanish, European attitudes toward work, and pride in the Spanish heritage.

Although numerically small, this group still has considerable influence in economics and politics. Their lifestyle includes all the modern luxuries, and with servants and large mansions or apartments, many enjoy a higher standard of living than most North Americans.

THE MESTIZOS

The *mestizos* are people of mixed Spanish and native blood. They make up about one-third of the Bolivian population. They are traditionally far more likely to speak and write Spanish than pure-blooded natives and therefore have found it easier to become part of mainstream Bolivian society.

Many people of mixed blood still make their living from selling handicrafts, trading, and running small businesses. However, since 1952, many mestizos have taken advantage of better educational opportunities, and now people of mixed blood are well established in all the major professions. Indeed, they have the reputation of being shrewd at business, and there are countless legends of the wealth of the mestizos. Other Bolivians believe that even the scruffy-looking mechanic who fixes their car probably has numerous deals on the fire and a fortune in the bank.

In modern Bolivian society, a few successful mestizos have even broken through Bolivia's strong class divide and become accepted into *blanco* society. At the same time, mestizo people often retain a respect for their native traditions and background.

Young city dwellers. Social position is determined by many other factors in addition to race, including people's ability to speak Spanish, whether they live in an urban area and work in a white-collar job, the way they act, and whether they wear European dress.

An Afro-Bolivan from the Yungas.

THE AFRO-BOLIVIANS

In the 16th century, the Spanish brought slaves from Africa to work in the mines. The Africans were unable to adjust to the cold Altiplano climate and were resettled in the Yungas, where they worked as farmers. Up until the 1952 revolution, their descendants were still working under near-slavery conditions. People alive today can remember being made to work in the fields when they were only 6 or 7 years old and being whipped if they did not work hard enough.

Today there are about 17,000 descendants of former slaves living in Bolivia. They speak Spanish with a sprinkling of African words, and those around La Paz are quite likely to speak Aymará as well. Some of the women have even copied the Aymará habit of wearing bowler hats.

Bolivians of African origin are still subject to subtle racism, with few of them attending college or holding influential positions. They have been able to make more of an impact in sports and music, and one of the few legacies of their African background is *saya* ("SIE-ah") music. Consisting of chants, dancing, and rhythmic drum beats, this African sound has been passed down from generation to generation. It has even crossed over into Bolivian mainstream culture. Saya rhythms and chants are used by fans at soccer matches.

In 1982, high school students in the Yungas created the Afro-Bolivian Cultural Movement to preserve their culture, and today special Afro-Bolivian concerts are often featured on national television.

NEW ARRIVALS

Over the years, Bolivia, with its great untapped potential, has attracted various waves of immigrants seeking a better life. The arrival of new groups has often resulted from upheavals in another part of the world. The persecution of Jews before and during World War II led to a large number of Polish and German immigrants coming to Bolivia. They tended to center in La Paz and Cochabamba, although many later moved on to Peru or Argentina.

Postwar poverty in Japan resulted in a group of Okinawan farmers immigrating to Santa Cruz. At first, life was very hard, and the new arrivals had to carve their homes out of the rainforest. The nearest town was two days away by horse, floods destroyed their first crops, and people died from the unhealthy forest climate.

Since then, the community has prospered, and today their small towns are home to nearly 2,000 people of Japanese background and twice as many Bolivians. The community has hospitals built with Japanese government aid, and Santa Cruz is now just a few hours away on a good road.

The Japanese immigrants introduced modern agricultural ideas to Bolivia, particularly rice growing and poultry farming. Today this small area produces half of Bolivia's poultry and eggs and enough rice to have a surplus for export.

The Okinawans still maintain their Japanese culture and language, and many of the children are sent to Japan for their university education.

Bolivia has a reputation of providing a safe haven for Nazi war criminals. Although many of the war criminal stories are based on rumors, Klaus Barbie, a Nazi Gestapo chief who conducted a reign of terror in South France, lived in Bolivia for several years.

Second- and third-generation Japanese-Bolivians tend to think of themselves as Bolivians, but with strong Japanese ties.

LIFESTYLE

LIFE IN THE RURAL AREAS OF BOLIVIA has not changed much since Incan times. This is particularly true on the Altiplano, the heartland of the country. Making a living in this harsh environment requires using all the resources available. The economy still centers around livestock.

There is a small variety of plants on the Altiplano, and virtually everything that grows is put to use. Thola and yareta are used for fuel, ichu is the main food for the llamas, and eucalyptus trees provide fuel and wood for house building and furniture.

One of the most useful plants is the totora reed, which grows around Lake Titicaca. These can be dried for fuel, fed to the livestock, or made into small boats. The boats are mainly used for fishing, and they last about a year before the reeds start to rot and the boat has to be replaced. Many people now have boats made from wood or fiberglass, and reed boat-making is becoming a dying art.

Llamas might look like harmless and cuddly animals, but they have nasty tempers and sometimes bite and spit at people who get too close.

Opposite: **The Aymará use totora reeds to thatch the roofs of their houses.**

Left: **Llamas are particularly important to highland farmers. They provide meat, wool, and leather, are used for transport, and their dried dung makes excellent fuel. Yet not every Altiplano family keeps a herd of llamas. Depending largely on the altitude they live at, farmers are just as likely to keep sheep and cattle and to use donkeys as beasts of burden.**

Beggars in La Paz. A rural drought in the 1980s brought waves of beggars into La Paz. Even after the drought was over, some stayed on in the city, and many now return each year. They can usually make enough money begging to purchase a few luxury items before returning to their village.

URBAN POOR

The 1952 revolution gave farmers the land they worked, but usually they have no paperwork for the property, so land cannot be sold. This means that farmers have to divide their land among their sons, so each generation the plots of land get smaller and the people poorer. As a result, many native farmers leave the countryside to seek work in the cities. The new arrivals stay with relations in the poorer neighborhoods, where the conditions are primitive, with little sanitation or heating.

Many people in the low-income groups work in factories or mines. The women become street traders, selling fruit, vegetables, or weavings, or even factory-made items ranging from plastic toys to computer disks.

Life for children in urban communities is worse than in rural areas, and young children often spend their days sitting on the street corner while their mothers work. Homeless and orphaned children sleep on the street and work as shoeshine boys or *voceadores* ("voh-say-ah-DOR-ays"). Voceadors work on the buses, shouting out stops and collecting fares.

COCA—PART OF LIFE

To most highland natives, the coca leaf is more than a luxury; it is an essential of life and survival would be hard without it. The leaves are a mild narcotic, and chewing them helps to numb cold, pain, and hunger. Coca is also used as a medicine.

According to legend, the natives once tried to burn a clearing to build their homes, but the fire got out of hand and burned down part of the forest. This made the gods angry, and they sent down a thunderstorm to put out the fire. By the time the storm was over, only one tough little plant, the coca, had survived. The people chewed the leaves and found it gave them nourishment and helped them forget the hardship they had brought upon themselves.

THE MINERS

Some mines are owned by the miners themselves and worked as cooperatives. Life is often hardest in these mines because there is little money to invest in equipment. Most of the work is done by hand, with miners working in narrow, unventilated, and unbearably hot passageways.

Although no one under the age of 18 is supposed to work in the mines, boys as young as 12 or 13 are sometimes taken on as helpers. After three or four years, they can apply to the cooperative to become miners.

Generally the miners gather early at the mine and linger outside, drinking tea and chewing coca to prepare themselves for the day ahead. Once underground, they may work for nine hours before returning to the surface. Miners in cooperative mines set their own dynamite to loosen the rock. It can take two or three hours just to chisel out a hole for the dynamite. After the explosion, the tunnel is full of dangerous fumes, and while waiting for these to disperse, the miners take a coca break. Miners believe that chewing coca not only gives them energy but also filters out some of the harmful fumes.

Miners in government mines are far better off, and they have a reputation for being very militant, often striking over conditions and sometimes getting involved in politics.

All miners, whether in co-operative or state-owned mines, have a hard and dangerous job. Even if they are lucky enough to avoid accidents, working in the mines almost inevitably leads to serious lung disease, and many miners die before they reach 50.

TRADITIONAL DRESS

The traditional native dress of homemade trousers and poncho is now seldom worn by men on the Altiplano; they are far more likely to wear factory-made trousers, jackets, and shirts. Traditional hats are even being replaced by baseball caps, although this fashion is popular so far only among boys and young men. For many people, *chullas* ("CHOO-yahs"), woolen caps with ear flaps, remain popular, if only because they are so practical in the cold weather.

Traditional dress is still widely worn by native women. Aymará women are reasonably uniform in their dress, but the Quechua show more variation, particularly in hats.

Traditional native dress for women consists of an apron over a long skirt with many underskirts. This makes the outer skirt stick out like a hoop skirt and keeps the women warm. They are worn with an embroidered blouse and a cardigan. The shawl, called a *mantu* ("MAHN-too") in Aymará, is a vital part of the outfit. These colorful rectangles can be folded to make a pouch at the back to carry shopping or babies. Home-woven cloth is now giving way to brightly colored factory-made material.

The final touch is a hat, which is very important on the Altiplano because it gives protection from the strong winds and fierce sun. Across Bolivia there is a wide range of headwear, but the favorite for Aymará women is the bowler hat, known locally as the *bombin* ("bohm-BEEN"). The bowler hat was first introduced to Bolivia by British railway workers, although why Aymará women rather than men started wearing them is a mystery. One story, probably only a legend, tells that a shipment of bowlers were sent to Bolivia by mistake and the owner sold them to the Aymará women by promising the hats would bring them fertility. For many years, the Borsalino factory in Italy made hats almost entirely for the Bolivian market, although today they are produced locally.

Women generally wear their hair in one long braid down the back.

HEALTH

Health is a major issue in Bolivia. The nation has a small budget for health care, and there are few doctors. On the average, Bolivian men live to be 59, and women 64. In the United States the same averages are 72 years for men and 79 for women. Infant mortality is also high, with 83 out of every 1,000 Bolivian babies dying. This compares with 10 out of 1,000 in the United States and 18 out of 1,000 in neighboring Argentina.

The government has put most of its limited resources into combating malaria

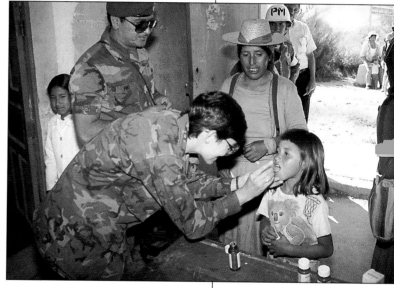

Military personnel operate a rural clinic. Poor hygiene and a lack of proper sanitation in the rural areas result in frequent dysentery and worm infections. In the lowlands, malaria is a constant danger. There was also a serious outbreak of yellow fever in the 1980s.

and dysentery, ignoring other diseases. Chagas disease, thought to infect anywhere between a million and four million Bolivians, has not received much attention. Chagas is caused by a bug that lives in cracked walls and roofs of poorly constructed homes. At night it bites people while they sleep. As it sucks blood, it leaves a dangerous parasite on the skin; if scratched, it works slowly into the bloodstream. There might be some immediate signs, such as fever or swelling, but these pass. The parasite, however, remains in the blood, and 15 or 20 years later, it attacks the heart and digestive system, resulting in what appears to be a sudden death.

BIRTH AND FAMILY PLANNING

In the past, family planning was largely ignored in Bolivia. Some private agencies worked with the rural population, but the government did not get involved. The present government has been more willing to consider the issue, and it acknowledges that family planning is important.

Traditionally, low-income Bolivian women breastfeed their children for a long period, sometimes up to two years. While they are breastfeeding, women are less likely to become pregnant again, and this has traditionally helped to space out the family. However, the increasing use of bottlefeeding disrupts this natural pattern.

Most poor people give birth at home, often without proper consideration for hygiene. Midwives, called *matronas* ("mah-TROH-nahs"), attend the mother. Although they are experienced, they have no medical training.

Urban women from higher income groups can either have their baby in a hospital or have a doctor in attendance at home. Family ties are so strong in Bolivia that it is not unusual for relations to wander in on women during labor, happily chat away, and then leave again.

PADRINOS

Padrinos ("pah-DREE-nohs"), or godparents, play a central role in Bolivian society. To be selected as a godparent is a great honor. Rich families use the padrino system to build ties with people of equal status. Poor people might ask someone of higher status, perhaps a boss at work, to be their child's padrino. A padrino who owns a factory could not refuse to give his godchild a job, nor could he see her miss school because she could not afford the textbooks. In rural areas, it is traditional for landowners, merchants, or politicians to accept many padrino commitments. This cements their position in society.

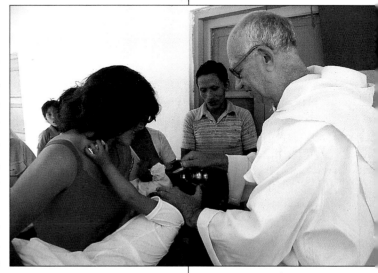

CHILDHOOD AND GROWING UP

The first years of childhood for many Bolivian children from low-income families are spent either strapped onto their mother's back or crawling around the ground playing while their mother works.

The hair cutting ceremony takes place at around 2 years of age, which is when many children are weaned. The child's hair is braided into lots of tiny pigtails, each tied with a ribbon. The first of these locks is cut by the padrinos. Other relations then take turns to cut a small piece of hair according to their age and rank in the family. Each person presents the child with a gift of money, which is pinned onto the child's clothes. In rural society, this money is used to buy animals. People say that crops may die, but livestock is capital for life. Herds of llamas or sheep are often tagged on the ear in different colors to mark which of the children in the family they belong to.

At 18 boys go off to do a year's service in the army. When they return, they are considered to have become men and, if their family can afford it, their safe return is celebrated with a large party.

BIRTHDAYS

Birthdays are big family occasions in Bolivia, and most people, whatever their age, have a party. It is important for adults to have the party on the exact day rather than wait for the weekend, even though parties tend to go on until late. A typical invitation for an adult party is for 6:00 in the evening, which means the first guest might arrive at about 8:00. Generally everybody brings their children along. There is dancing, probably a meal around 11:00, and the cutting of the cake at midnight.

It is common to celebrate a child's birthday on the weekend, usually on a Saturday, starting around noon. There are light refreshments, probably *salteñas* ("sal-TAY-nyahs"), and perhaps hot dogs, because many children do not like the spicy salteñas. Most people bring a small gift to the party—a toy for children or chocolates or a bottle of wine for adults. The gifts are wrapped and are put aside to be opened later. As Bolivian people do not usually put their names on these gifts, the person having a birthday usually never learns who gave what present.

WEDDINGS

In the countryside, it is common for people to live together, usually in the man's family house, before marrying. Generally after a festival, the man will persuade the woman to move in with him. This is called "stealing the girl." In the days that follow, the two families meet and negotiate the union, and then exchange gifts. The couple might stay together for years and have children before they have saved enough for a wedding with a priest and a celebration with their family and neighbors.

In urban areas, Aymará, Quechua, and mestizo weddings are a great occasion. Saturday is the traditional day to get married. After the service, the couple wait on the church steps, and the guests take turns offering congratulations. The bride and groom then climb into a taxi that has been specially chartered and decorated for the occasion. The best man jumps into the front seat and the parents into the back until there are six or seven people inside, not including the driver. The other guests climb into a waiting bus, and the wedding party reassembles at a local hall for the party.

A wedding procession. It is traditional in rural society for the couple to lead a procession from the church to the bride's home for a banquet.

Schoolchildren in Bolivia. The middle classes place considerable emphasis on education, whereas in rural communities the dropout rate is high.

EDUCATION

Education in Bolivia is free, universal, and compulsory. However, children in rural communities are also expected to do their share of the work on the farm, so many children drop out of school before finishing their elementary education at the age of 14. Classes are in Spanish, which most indigenous children find difficult to understand. It is impossible to get exact figures, but probably somewhere between 60% and 85% of primary school age children attend school.

Secondary school lasts four years but is not compulsory, and only around a third of the population continue in school beyond primary school. Most secondary schools are located in towns and cities, so it is very difficult for rural children to attend. Some families arrange for sons to go and live in the town with another family. That family virtually owns the boy, who must work for them when he comes back from school. It is a very hard system but does allow a few boys from rural backgrounds to graduate. Most rural families will not permit their

EDUCATIONAL REFORM

The Bolivian government is now attempting to reform the education system. Starting in 1995, 300 schools around the country pioneered the experiment. The aim of the new reforms is to introduce teaching in the children's native language and encourage esteem for the different cultures. The reforms also provide libraries and other facilities that many primary schools lack.

The Chipaya consider themselves the oldest race in the world and are known as "the people of the tombs." This is because of the houses, or chullpas ("CHOOL-pahs"), where they keep the skeletons of their ancestors.

daughters to live away from home, which denies them the chance of a secondary education.

Probably only one in five Bolivian adults can read, and this figure varies drastically between the different racial and social classes. However, the literacy rate is improving throughout Bolivian society.

FUNERALS

Three o'clock is the preferred time for a funeral. It has been said that funerals are the only events in Bolivia that start on time. Funerals are an emotional affair with a great deal of sobbing and visible grief. After the service, close friends carry the coffin out of the church and then walk two or three blocks, with the other guests following. After a set distance, the coffin is put in a hearse for the rest of the journey to the cemetery.

A cemetery in La Paz.

Poor families find the money to pay for a funeral for an adult, even if they have to borrow it. However, child mortality is high, and a child's funeral might take a different format. A member of the family is sent to buy a casket while the family washes and dresses the child's body. They use their own candles and flowers to decorate the room.

It is usual to let other children climb onto the table to touch and kiss the body because this is their way of saying goodbye and understanding what has happened.

ROLE OF WOMEN

The rights of women are well protected by Bolivian law, but cultural and social traditions continue to hold women back, and Bolivia remains a chauvinist society.

Women do not always benefit from the laws that are there to protect them. For example, Bolivian women are entitled to three months' maternity leave. However, many women in low-paying jobs are unaware of this or afraid of losing their jobs if they do take the time off.

From childhood, native women are brought up to be passive and

For working class women, life is likely to consist of continual hard work and giving birth to children.

A WOMAN FOR THE NINETIES

Monica Medina de Palenque is a politician to watch in the future. She was a highly successful ballet dancer who trained in Madrid and danced with the Spanish National Ballet Company. She returned to Bolivia in 1984 and married the folksinger Carlos Palenque Aviles, who is often cited as a possible future president. They both starred in television and radio shows in which they gave poor people a chance to air their grievances.

Disenchanted with the current political parties, they formed their own party, CONDEPA. In 1993, Monica Medina was elected the first woman mayor of La Paz.

conservative, and although they make a major contribution to the economy, they generally remain subordinate to their fathers and husbands. As a result, they rarely get the chance to participate in the village meetings where decisions are made or to benefit from training programs. If they are widowed, it can be difficult for them to run the farm on their own because officials are sometimes reluctant to give them the important agricultural credits.

Less emphasis is placed on educating girls; some 89% of boys of primary school age are sent to school but only 81% of girls.

Women are often subjected to domestic violence. In the countryside, much of this goes unreported, but in the cities, it is now becoming far more of an issue. There is even a television program that publicizes cases of domestic violence each week and puts the victims in contact with lawyers.

In middle-class society, women have previously remained largely economically inactive. This is changing rapidly, and more and more Bolivian women are moving into high-profile leadership roles.

La Paz schoolgirls. Even in established urban families, where all children are likely to be sent to school, it is common for parents to send their sons to better private schools and their daughters to government schools.

71

RELIGION

WHEN THE SPANISH ARRIVED in Bolivia, they brought the Roman Catholic religion with them, and today 95% of the population are Catholic. However, Catholicism is mixed with indigenous beliefs, which still have a strong hold in the indigenous communities. Bolivian people say that they have one foot in the church and one foot in tradition.

In the last 30 years, the Roman Catholic Church has ventured into the fields of social work and education. Under some of the more oppressive dictators, the church has often been a powerful voice speaking up for human rights. In 1980, Archbishop Jorge Manrique of La Paz opened an office to help political prisoners, and a Catholic newspaper was banned.

About 1.4% of the population follow the Protestant faith, which includes Methodists, Episcopalians, Baptists, and Jehovah's Witnesses. The Protestant faiths are gaining ground in the Aymará community.

The churches are important landmarks, and the squares in front of them form a meeting place and trading center. In the cities, Bolivian churches are generally active places, with people continually coming and going.

Opposite: **A woman praying inside the cathedral in Copacabana. People pray before a favorite statue, light candles, or just sit and meditate.**

Left: **The church of Toledo.**

Incas worshipping the sun. As they conquered other cultures, the Incas did not necessarily suppress their religions, but they demanded that Inti rule over the local gods.

THE INCAN RELIGION

Before the Spanish arrived, the Incas had their own religion. They believed in many different gods, built temples to honor them, and trained priests to oversee the worship. There is a great deal we do not know about the Incan religion, but it seems to have been a combination of nature worship, theological notions, animistic beliefs, and magic.

The supreme god was Inti, the sun god. The emperor was seen as the son of Inti, so that worship of Inti was tied in with worshipping the emperor. Inti's wife was Mamaquilla, the moon goddess. Pachamama ruled over the earth, Coha was the mother of the sea, and Illampu was the god of thunder and rain.

The earth was created by Viracocha, who made the first giants, and when he was unhappy with them, turned them into stone. He then came out of Lake Titicaca to create a new race of humans. Later on, Viracocha appears to have become more important than Inti. Various historians have tried to guess the reasons for this development.

The agricultural seasons were particularly important to the Incas, and great religious festivals were held at all the important stages of the farming season. People were expected to provide food and labor for the gods, and there were sacrifices of animals. Human sacrifices also took place, particularly at times of stress, but this was a serious event and conducted only in the main temples.

THE OLD GODS SURVIVE

The old gods, who date back to pre-Spanish times, are still part of the Bolivian culture. Whether people believe in them as gods, as superstition, or simply as part of their folklore that they wish to keep alive is debatable.

There is certainly a serious respect for Pachamama, the Incan earth mother, which Quechua society associates with the Virgin Mary. Pachamama protects people, animals, and plants but can also be cruel and revengeful. Pachamama presides over all major events, such as marriages or giving birth, but she must also be considered when it comes to more mundane actions, such as chewing the first coca of the day.

Pachamama has the first right to all things, and whenever people start drinking alcohol, a little liquid is poured on the ground for her. People of native origin carefully place a little chewed coca on the road as an offering before undertaking a journey. She is also honored when the first furrows are dug, and at the completion of a new building.

Ekeko, which means "dwarf" in Aymará, is a pleasant little household god who retains a role in Bolivian daily life. Figurines of Ekeko portray him as a round-faced, grinning little figure laden with kitchen items. He is responsible for finding wives and husbands, for good luck in business, and for providing homes. He is particularly revered in mestizo culture.

El Tío ("TEE-oh") is the ruler of hell and owner of minerals. Miners place small ceramic figures of El Tío in niches in the passageways into their mine. This figure is offered coca, cigarettes, and alcohol to keep him happy. He is never referred to as the devil, but always as *Tío*, which means "uncle."

INFLUENCE OF THE JESUITS

For many years, the government in the high plateau had little interest in the lowlands. Instead, this area was developed by Jesuit priests, who came across the border from Paraguay. They set up around 30 communities throughout the region, each with a few priests to run them and a contingent of soldiers for protection.

The Jesuits were quite zealous in imposing their type of Catholicism on the native population, and in doing so they destroyed much of the culture that had once existed in this region. In its place they introduced Spanish culture, and this still shows in the local music, which is quite different from anywhere else in Bolivia.

The Jesuit communities were well run and prosperous. The priests grew cotton, sugarcane, corn, yucca, rice, and many other fruits and vegetables. They also brought in cattle and horses. Trade grew between the lowlands and the highlands. Sugarcane, other crops, and finished works of art were exchanged for silver. The missions and their armed forces also protected the local people from Brazilian slave traders.

For many years, the area was virtually an autonomous religious state, forming a buffer zone between the Spanish and Portuguese in South America. Eventually the Jesuits become too powerful, and the Spanish kings started to become suspicious of their activities and jealous of their wealth. In 1767, all Jesuit priests were expelled from the continent.

The Jesuit church in Santa Cruz. The Jesuits gave the indigenous people the opportunity of having an education and also taught many practical skills. The region became famous for its wood carvings and other works of art.

MIRACLES AND PILGRIMAGES

In the small village of Quillacollo in 1770, the youngest daughter of a poor family had the task of looking after the sheep. One day, while out in the fields, she met a beautiful woman holding a little baby. The young girl and the woman met many times, and the daughter so enjoyed their talks that she often returned home late.

Her family did not believe her story, so one day they followed her. Seeing her parents, the daughter cried out "Orko pena," which in the Quechua language means "she is on the hill." With this cry, the woman and baby disappeared before the eyes of the startled parents. The news spread around the village, and the people who rushed to the spot found a small image of the Virgin Mary. Today that image is in the village church, and every year on August 15, it is paraded around the village.

There is an important pilgrimage to Copacabana each year. The town is overlooked by a tall, steep hill called the Cerro Calvario, which has been marked out with the stations of the cross. At dusk on Good Friday, there is a candlelight procession from the cathedral to the top of the hill.

Pilgrims to the Cerro Calvario place stones on each cross and at the top pray and burn incense. They also leave miniature models of items they hope to acquire in the months ahead. Some people even walk the 90 miles (150 kilometers) from La Paz as part of this pilgrimage.

CHA'LLA

A *cha'lla* ("CHAY-ya") is a ritual blessing. It might be a Christian event, a ceremony drawn from native folklore, or as is often the case, a combination of the two. It is conducted by a *yatiri* ("yah-TEE-ree") or a Christian priest.

A cha'lla ceremony is performed whenever a new building is completed, otherwise there will never be peace in that building. The ceremony takes place on a Saturday. The owner of the builidng and the workers prepare an offering, called a *cucho* ("KOO-choh"), of a wax man, grains of incense, aromatic herbs, a few leaves of coca, cotton still on the branch, tin figures of humans and animals, and household objects, all sprinkled with wine. One of the workers acts as the holy man for the ceremony. He is left alone with the cucho, which he burns. He watches the way the smoke rises to be sure all the evil spirits have left. He also asks Pachamama for her blessing. When the others return, the ashes from the offerings and any chewed coca are placed in a sack and buried in the foundations. From then on, the cucho is the invisible guardian of the building.

WITCHCRAFT AND WISDOM

The *yatiri* is the local witch doctor who can be hired to help with problems. Yatiri often conduct services very much like a priest. If you were visiting a holy place, you might ask a yatiri to conduct a small service first. The yatiri will burn incense, sing chants, and make an offering to Pachamama to make sure your visit goes smoothly. If you want advice on a marriage or a business venture, you might ask a yatiri to tell your fortune. A fortune is often predicted by reading coca leaves. The fortune teller talks to the spirits, and then spreads a handful of leaves on a cloth to look for clues about the future from the shape they form. Fortune telling in this way might also be used to find lost items or people.

Amautu ("ah-MOW-too") are wise men. In Incan society, the amautu had to remember vast amounts of information because there were no written records. They are still respected for their wisdom.

Many people believe in harmful spirits. *Karisirus* are night phantoms who catch people out after dark or when they are sleeping. According to legend, they split their victim's stomach and extract some of the fat.

La Paz has a whole street known as the witches' market, where they sell herbs, seeds, and various animal parts, including llama fetus, which should be placed under the cornerstone of any new building.

In rural areas, mothers calling their children indoors shout a warning about the karisirus to make them come home quicker.

LANGUAGE

BOLIVIA HAS THREE OFFICIAL LANGUAGES: Spanish, Aymará, and Quechua. In addition, there are dozens of isolated languages that are each spoken by a few thousand people. Various waves of immigrants have also added to this mixture. In a few lowland towns, you could probably communicate just as easily in Japanese as in Spanish.

Although the Aymará and Quechua languages have acquired a new status, Spanish remains the most important language of commerce, art, broadcasting, and politics. However, less than half of the population speak Spanish as their first language, and it is estimated that 40% of Bolivians cannot read or speak Spanish at all. This reinforces racial inequalities in Bolivia.

Opposite: **Spanish is the language used for road signs and newspapers.**

Below: **Public typists set up shop on the sidewalk.**

Two native men conversing.

QUECHUA AND AYMARÁ

Bolivia's other two official languages are Quechua and Aymará. These two languages are quite similar in technical points, such as the way words are compounded, so linguists believe they might be related. Indeed, someone who does not speak either language might listen to them and think they were the same. The vocabulary, however, is very different, and Quechua and Aymará speakers cannot understand each other.

In the past, few Spanish speakers bothered to learn either of the Andean languages, preferring that the native population learn Spanish. With interest increasing in native culture, this situation is slowly changing. However, even Spanish speakers who are willing to try to learn one of their nation's other official languages do not necessarily find it easy to do so. The sound of both Aymará and Quechua is very different from most European languages, and this makes them difficult for Spanish speakers to learn. There are also other differences. For example, the power and force with which some sounds are delivered are an important part of the communication, as is leaving a slight pause between some sounds.

The media do little to cater to Aymará and Quechua speakers, although radio and television do give the news in the two indigenous languages. These programs are usually broadcast early in the morning, before the farming community starts work. The radio program even carries personal messages, uniting family members who live far apart.

HOW SIMILAR THEY ARE?

Here are the numbers one to ten in Aymará and Quechua. Can you see if they look similar to each other?

	Aymará	Quechua
one	ma	hoq
two	payai	iskay
three	quimsa	kinsa
four	pusit	tawa
five	pesca	pisqa
six	htaso	soqta
seven	pakalkok	qanchis
eight	quimsa	pusag
nine	yatun	isqon
ten	tunca	chunka

The Jesuit missionary Ludovico Bertonio, who wrote the first Aymará-Spanish dictionary in 1610, described it as a "genius of a language." It is a well thought out language, with simple, easy-to-understand rules.

QUECHUA Quechua was the language of the Incan empire and, as a result, is still spoken by 13 million native people in Peru, Bolivia, Ecuador, Chile, and northwest Argentina. This makes it an important international language. Because it covers such a wide area and so many different groups, Quechua has many different dialects. Some Quechua speakers would understand each other only with difficulty.

Recently, scholars have come up with the idea of writing out common rules and vocabulary to unify the language. However, Quechua is largely an oral language with little written tradition.

AYMARÁ The Aymará people retained their language despite attempts to suppress it by both the Incas and the Spanish. Today it is spoken by about 2.5 million people in Peru and Bolivia. It is a harsh, guttural-sounding language, with sounds coming from the back of the throat.

It is said that 4,000 years ago a group of wise men sat down and made up the language from scratch. Recently a Bolivian mathematician, Ivan Guzmán de Rojas, has been creating computer programs that use Aymará to translate European languages because of its simplicity and clarity.

BEWARE THE FALSE FRIENDS

Many Spanish and English words look and sound the same. There are two reasons for this. Some words are similar because they originally came from the same Latin root. Other words have been borrowed from the other language. For example, Spanish has given the English language words such as *alligator, tomato, guitar, cork, armada*, and *vanilla*. A few words have even passed from Aymará or Quechua to Spanish, and from there to English. The best example of this is *llama*.

However, Spanish also has many words that look the same as English words but have a different meaning. For example, *la carpeta* might be thought to mean the carpet, but in fact it means "folder." *Jubilacion* is not the Spanish word for "jubilation," but means "retirement." Such words are called false friends and are something people have to be aware of when learning Spanish.

Reading the newspaper. There are five daily newspapers in La Paz, of which the largest is the Catholic *Presencia*.

SPANISH

Spanish is one of the Romance languages, which means it originated from Latin. A version of vulgar Latin was first brought to Spain by Roman soldiers and settlers, and over the centuries, it underwent many other influences until, by the Middle Ages, a distinctive Spanish language had emerged.

When the Spanish built up their great colonial empire they introduced their language to regions they conquered. As a result, some 300 million people around the world now speak Spanish as a first language, and businesspeople from Cuba, Bolivia, and Spain could quite happily communicate with each other in their common language. Spanish is also one of the official languages of the United Nations.

The Spanish spoken in Bolivia is slower than what you hear in Spain, and Bolivian people do not drop syllables as much. Some of the sounds are also different. The *z* and *ci* in words such as *gracias* and *manzana* are pronounced as a *th* sound in Spain but as an *s* sound in Bolivia.

The Bolivian language has adopted many words from the Andean languages. A few native words were taken back to Spain by the colonialists and are now incorporated into mainstream Spanish.

NONVERBAL COMMUNICATION

Bolivian people of European background make great use of their hands when talking. They often make contact with each other, touching arms or shoulders to emphasize an important point.

The indigenous highland people are far less expressive. Even when arguing, they remain immobile and refrain from shouting. Instead, the two people having the dispute talk simultaneously and continuously in a low, agitated voice.

When people meet, it is very common for men to greet women, and women to greet other women, with a single kiss on the cheek. Two men meeting limit their contact to a handshake and maybe an embrace. Strangers do not kiss on the first meeting, but if they build a bond, they might kiss the next time they meet.

Indigenous people greeting each other are far more formal. At weddings or family gatherings, they shake hands and, at the same time, gently pat each other's shoulder with their free hand. They often lean forward as they do this, making it look as if they were about to kiss, but then changed their minds. Indigenous people shake hands very lightly.

Spanish Bolivians gesture a lot when talking. Sometimes their free hand seems to be moving continually, as if conducting the conversation.

Bolivian people are quite open about touching, and men and women often walk down the street arm in arm. This is a particularly strong practice between fathers and daughters.

ARTS

BOLIVIA HAS A SURPRISINGLY diverse and rich culture. Music and dance are particularly strong, but Bolivian painters and sculptors have also produced some remarkable work.

There is a National Academy of Fine Arts in La Paz, which promotes music, painting, sculpture, and ceramics.

However, Bolivia is isolated from the rest of the world, so only a very few Bolivian writers or artists have attracted much attention outside the country. Many of these have only done so by moving overseas, particularly to the United States. One pleasing trend is that many of the best artists, who fled during the military dictatorships, are now returning to Bolivia.

Bolivia also has a rich heritage of folk art and handicrafts, which includes the costumes and masks created for fiestas.

People often seek to identify links between contemporary Bolivian art and the traditional work of the indigenous population. Although the native community has had some influence, particularly in music and dance, artists and writers have tended to be influenced more by their contemporaries in other Latin American countries.

Since World War II, the United States has also had an increasing influence on Bolivian art. With the arrival of satellite television, Bolivia's own culture might well have to compete against a great many more outside influences in the years to come.

Many native women weave shawls both to wear and to sell to tourists to supplement the family income *(opposite).* **The finished product may look like this beautiful shawl** *(above).*

There is a series of festival dances that the native people created to make fun of the Spanish. In the past, it was only at fiesta time that such "insolence" was tolerated by the colonialists, and now these dances have become part of the fiesta tradition.

DANCE

The folk dances that are performed today are a combination of pre-Hispanic dances, Spanish dances, and African dances brought to Bolivia by the slaves. The most famous, and the nearest Bolivia has to a national folk dance, is the *cueca* ("KWAY-kah"), or handkerchief dance. The cueca can trace its roots through the Chilean cueca to the Spanish fandango. The dance opens with an introduction, during which the partners look at each other provocatively, building up the tension. On the call of *adentro* ("ah-DEN-troh"), the couple start to dance, partners whirling around each other, linking arms at times, and waving their handkerchiefs in spirals above their heads with their free hand. This stage of the dance symbolizes the man trying to win the woman, who escapes from him. During the second stage, the dance becomes softer and more gentle as the partners come to an agreement. The final stage of the dance is preceded by the cry of *zapateo* ("zah-pah-TAY-oh"). This is a repeat of the first stage, but with more force. At this point the spectators start clapping in time with the beat.

VISUAL ARTS

The Incas were magnificent artists, but their best work in gold and silver was melted down by the Spaniards. Modern Bolivian art started with the colonial period, and the first artwork was religious. The most renowned artist of this period was Melchor Pérez de Holguín, who was born in 1660. His religious paintings contain many strange touches. In one painting, a saint talks to an angel while in the background an alien-looking bird attacks a frog.

Church authorities employed mestizo artists, and in the 17th and 18th centuries, a mestizo baroque style developed that mixed native and Spanish styles.

The fathers of contemporary Bolivian art are Cecilio Guzmán de Rojas and Arturo Borda. Guzmán studied in Madrid, returning to Bolivia in 1929. He was one of the first painters to portray native subjects, and Machu Picchu in Peru was a favorite theme. He also depicted the beauty and nobility of the indigenous Andean people. His style was influenced by cubism.

Borda abandoned painting for a long period of his life, preferring to work as an actor. When he returned to painting, he covered a wide range of subjects. A favorite subject was Mount Illimani, which he painted from all angles and in all different kinds of light.

Women artists have had much success. María Núñez del Prado creates sculptures from natural materials that are heavily influenced by the native culture. María Luisa Pacheco was a student of Guzmán but spent most of her career in the United States.

Typical folk painting of the Aymará.

Panpipes are a traditional instrument in Andean folk music.

TRADITIONAL MUSIC

Much of Bolivia's traditional music is based on simple instruments that boys play to pass the long hours while they are looking after the animals. As a result, every village, even every street, usually has its own band.

Although the music and dance of the Altiplano are considered representative of Bolivia, in fact there is a remarkable degree of regional variation. The music of the cold, harsh Altiplano tends to be sad and mournful, but in the lowlands music is faster and more lively. Chaco music is the most distinctive and concentrates more on violin, drum, and guitar. This is largely due to the influence of Jesuit priests, who taught the people to play European instruments.

The most important recent trend is to introduce lyrics to the mournful Andean music, creating a new genre of folksongs. Folk musicians have the opportunity to play in street festivals, and the best groups might be invited to perform at a *peñas* ("PAY-nyas"). These are folk music shows that take place in restaurants.

Los Kjarkas is the best known of the Bolivian folk groups and plays a stylized kind of modern folk song. Other well-known groups include Savia Andina, who have used their music to protest conditions in Bolivia, and Wara, considered the best of the traditional Aymará groups.

Despite a growing influence from the western music that is carried into the remotest homes by radio, traditional Bolivian folk music still remains the most popular.

MUSICAL INSTRUMENTS

Traditional Bolivian instruments generally come in families of small, large, and medium-sized instruments. Most typical are the simple flutes made from reed pipes, which are known as *quenas* ("KAY-nas"), and the more complicated *zampoña* ("zahm-POH-nya").

The quena (shown above) does not have a mouthpiece, but is played by blowing into a notch at one end. Traditionally it was a solo instrument, but it is now often incorporated into a musical ensemble. The recognized master of the reed flute is Gilbert Fabre.

Zampoñas, also known as panpipes, or by the Aymará name of *siku* ("SEE-koo"), are more complicated and consist of a collection of different-sized reeds lashed together. The sound is produced by forcing air across the open end of the reeds. It is the zampoña that gives musical troupes much of their distinctive sound.

Shells and cowhorns might also be used, and drums have also become a central part of Andes music, although many of the designs are based on Spanish military drums. String instruments include the *churrango* ("chuh-RAN-goh"), a small, guitar-like instrument made from an armadillo shell. Unlike the guitar, it has 10 strings arranged in pairs, and the best churrangos are prized works of art. Another string instrument is the *violin chapaco*, a variation of the European violin.

The National Symphony Orchestra has recently found new energy and is putting on many exciting programs under the guidance of the young conductor, Freddy Terrazas. Terrazas is a good example of the talented artists who are returning to Bolivia.

MODERN MUSIC

The Spanish had a major influence on South American music, including introducing the guitar, the piano, the military-style brass band, and the symphony orchestra. All these forms of music-making are popular in Bolivia, particularly the brass bands that regularly play at weddings or religious occasions.

Bolivia has produced some extremely talented musicians. Pianist Wálter Ponce was the winner of the Queen Elizabeth of Belgium award, an international competition for the world's best young musicians. Ana María Vera was the youngest pianist to be invited to perform at the Kennedy Center In Washington, D.C.

Alberto Villal Pando is considered the country's leading contemporary composer. His music is inspired by Altiplano and traditional music, and he is now working on an opera set in colonial Potosí. Fidel Torricos works with cueca and other popular dance music.

Some of the most popular musicians are churrango players. The very best players, such as Mauro Núñez and his students Jaime Torres, Celestino Campos, and Ernesto Cavour, are famous throughout Bolivia.

The strength of Bolivia's musical tradition has made it harder for some forms of music to become accepted. Johnny Gonzalez is a jazz singer with an international reputation, but he has had to struggle to get people to listen to him in his own country. After studying in the La Paz Conservatory, Gonzalez went to France, where he played with Duke Ellington. Gonzalez left Bolivia in the 1970s, disillusioned with the political situation, but has recently been returning to his homeland to try to increase interest in jazz.

MOVIES

In the 1960s and 1970s, Bolivian movies came to international attention with the work of two major directors, Antonio Eguino and Jorge Sanjines. This was the period of "militant cinema," when movies looked at Bolivia's problems, particularly the plight of the indigenous people. Sanjines' most famous movie is perhaps *Blood of the Condor*. It is a chilling story of American doctors who sterilize native women who come to their clinic. When the village people realize what is happening, they attack the doctors and are then murdered by the Bolivian army.

Several locally made movies hit the screen in 1994, including *Viva Bolivia Toda La Vida*, a movie set to the background of the Bolivian team playing in the World Cup soccer match.

One of Eguino's best known movies is *Chuquiago*, which follows four overlapping stories in different social classes in La Paz.

Because of the way the cinema has championed the cause of the nation's poor and highlighted problems in the social system, military governments have often cracked down on the movie industry, and Sanjines himself has spent several years in exile.

During the last few years, Bolivian cinema has become even more active. Sanjines has recently produced *La Nación Clandestina*, which tells the story of an Aymará man's life in the city.

LITERATURE

Gabriel René-Moreno left a wonderful description of life in early Bolivia in spite of an overly procolonial view. Franz Tamayo, who lived between 1879 and 1956, was the first writer to champion the cause of the native people. Particularly in his poems, he describes the nobility of the natives, a most unusual view at the time for an aristocrat. In 1935, Tamayo was elected president, but a coup prevented him from taking office.

Another writer to take up the rights of the native population was Alcides Arguedas, who was born in the same year as Tamayo. Arguedas' main novels, *Wata Wara* and *Raza de Bronce,* brought him fame throughout Latin America. Jesús Lara, who wrote about native peasant life, is one of the few Bolivian authors to be widely read outside the country.

The most outstanding modern author is José Wolfango Montes Vannuchi who, in 1987, published his highly acclaimed novel, *Jonah and the Pink Whale.* This is a very funny account of life in the boom town of Santa Cruz.

FOLK ART

It is said that in Bolivia the best art is not found in museums, but on the streets. There is certainly a rich heritage of folk art, particularly weaving. Bolivian weaving is considered to be of a particularly high quality. First the wool is spun on a small spindle into a single strand. It is then transferred to a larger spindle and spun into a two-ply yarn. After being dyed, it is given a third spin. It is this third spin that gives Bolivian cloth its strength, elasticity, and hard, smooth surface.

A native weaving shows the inventiveness of design of native Bolivians.

Native women spend long hours spinning or weaving on heddle looms, and the textiles they produce come in many varied styles and patterns, with considerable regional influences. The best textiles are generally considered to be the red and black designs from the town of Potolo. One modern influence is the increased use of the less expensive sheep's wool rather than that of llama and alpaca.

Other well-developed forms of folk art include musical instruments, particularly the churrango, masks, and silver jewelry.

A BOLIVIAN VILLAGE TAKES ON THE ART DEALERS

The Incas wove beautiful textiles in vibrant colors. The oldest and finest cloths came from Coromo, where the people believed the cloths contained the souls of their ancestors. The cloths were only brought out on the day of the dead, but unscrupulous people took advantage of this festival to photograph the cloths. Many of the cloths were later stolen by Bolivians, who sold them to rich collectors in the United States.

There did not seem to be any way that a poor remote Bolivian village could take on the rich New York art dealers, but thanks to wide publicity and support from groups in the United States, several of the stolen cloths have now been returned to the village.

LEISURE

HOLIDAYS AND WEEKENDS IN BOLIVIA are a time to spend with friends and family, reinforcing ties and bonds and enjoying each other's company. On special occasions, such as weddings or festivals, family gatherings involve a considerable amount of singing, dancing, and feasting. At other times, such as on a quiet weekend, time together is more likely to be spent lingering over a leisurely meal with the traditional conversation hour afterward.

In cities, public parks form an important part of the social life. The park is a place where children play football and volleyball and ride their bikes. Adults sit in the sun talking, and teenage couples cuddle together on a bench, ignoring everybody else around them. Generally when adults sit in the park, they seem happy enough just to pass the time in conversation, but groups of men might play cards or dice.

In addition, many people belong to special dance clubs that spend months practicing to give displays at the major

festivals. Members of dance teams might also spend several hundred dollars on their elaborate costumes.

For native women, free time is largely spent knitting or weaving. Even when walking along the street, women are often spinning wool. Partly this might be considered work because many of the items they make will be sold for extra income. However, the women also get a great deal of pleasure and pride from their handicraft.

Opposite: **A street cinema offers a variety of films for viewing, including Bruce Lee.**

Above: **Feeding the pigeons in La Paz.**

97

CHILDREN'S GAMES

Many Bolivian children have little money to spend on toys, and they have to improvise their own games. An old bicycle wheel will become a hoop, a pile of stones building bricks.

The most popular game of all is spinning tops, and small wooden tops are for sale in every market. The game is wildly played by boys from the ages of 7 or 8 through the early teenage years.

Marbles, using factory-made glass marbles, is another popular game. The players each place a marble in a circle drawn in the dirt. They then flick a second marble into the arena. From this point on, players win any marble they hit with their marble. Although simple, the game has many additional rules that the boys playing all seem to understand.

Other common street games include clapping games, chase games, and games played with stones, where players try to throw their stones as close to a mark on the ground as possible. In the rural areas, slingshots made from a forked tree branch and old elastic are popular. This game allows boys to practice their skill and is useful in scaring birds off the crops.

However, children are often discouraged from playing because in Bolivian society playing is associated with being lazy. In the rural areas, it is thought that children should be working on the farm, and in middle class homes, they are expected to be doing their homework.

When children spin tops, they probably do not realize that they are playing a game that has been enjoyed in Bolivia since Incan times, when it was known as *pisqoynyo* ("pees-COIN-yo"). The favorite game is to spin the top and then slide two fingers underneath it and try to pick it up while it is still spinning. Once the top is in their hand, the children try to drop it onto an upturned bottle cap.

TRADITIONAL SPORTS

Apart from soccer, which is played nearly everywhere, sports are largely an activity for the urban population. For the majority of Bolivians in the countryside, life is too hard to leave much energy or enthusiasm for sports.

Bolivia does have a few traditional sports. *Tinku* ("TEEN-koo"), which takes place on festival days, is a bare-fisted type of boxing that starts off as a ritual dance and usually breaks down into a free-for-all in which the contestants try to knock each other down by any means possible. Fists and feet fly, and the whole event is a great favorite with crowds. Indeed, as people get more and more excited, the violence often spills over into the audience. This modern version is tame compared with earlier versions, when the boys taking part used slings to throw cacti at each other.

There is also a yearly swimming race across the narrowest part of Lake Titicaca. The distance is not particularly long, but the water is extremely cold, making it a test of endurance for the competitors.

Some villages also arrange bullfights. These are not the Spanish type of bullfight, but rather are staged between two prize bulls who are brought together in an open field. After much pawing of the ground, the two animals lock horns in battle, to the delight of the cheering crowd, who are generally sensible enough to keep a fair distance away.

A neighborhood soccer game. Soccer is very popular in Bolivia, either to play or to watch. In one village, everyone had gathered around the television to watch a World Cup game and were so engrossed in the match that no one noticed a fire had broken out until half the houses had burned down!

A NATION OF SOCCER LOVERS

Soccer is the national sport of Bolivia and is played on every street corner and park. Supporters show their loyalty to the best teams by placing stickers in their cars or by wearing replicas of their favorite team's shirts.

Important games are played at the national stadium in La Paz, where the home team always has a great advantage due to the altitude. Despite this, Bolivia has lost most of its international games. The most notable exception came in 1963, when the national team won the South American Championship in their own high-altitude stadium.

In the 1994 World Cup qualifying tournament, the Bolivian team notched up a whole series of good results. They beat the Brazilians 2-0, Uruguay 3-1, and then traveled to Venezuela, where they hit seven goals past the home team. These victories helped Bolivia become one of the 24 nations to qualify for the World Cup finals in the United States. Just getting to the World Cup was a great achievement, and success on the soccer field was seen as symbolic of the new mood in the nation.

Bolivia has a professional league for their strongest clubs. Traditionally, the best teams are Jorge Wilstermann, Bolívar, and The Strongest. However, this old hierarchy is being challenged. Teams from the lowlands, such as Blooming and Oriente Petrolero, are receiving sponsorship from the oil companies and are now able to attract some of the best players.

Soccer is not just a game for professional players. Hundreds of men, but very few women, play for recreation. The better players might belong to local teams who have team uniforms and play on full size fields, although they will generally be mud or sand rather than grass. Less serious players join casual games in the park. These games are usually played on a concrete arena the size of a basketball court, with four or five players on each team. The games end when the first goal is scored, the winners staying to play the next opponents.

The star Bolivian soccer player is Marco Antonio Etcheverry, known as *El Diablo*, who plays for a top club in Chile. He is famous for both his skill and his wild temper.

THE WORLD'S MOST FAMOUS SOCCER SCHOOL

In 1978, businessman Rolando Aguilera had the idea of opening up a soccer school for the poor children of the city of Santa Cruz. On the first day, 250 children arrived at the gate of Tahuichi Academy, and since then thousands have benefited from the academy's work.

Tahuichi's best teams have won youth tournaments all over the world, and 50 of their graduates now play for professional clubs.

However, Tahuichi Academy has always been primarily interested in the children themselves, and soccer is merely a tool to give them pride and a purpose in life. The academy therefore also oversees the children's health, nutrition, and education.

OTHER SPORTS

Bolivians play many different sports, and every four years they send a small team to the Olympic Games. However, they have yet to win a medal. Even in the South American Games, Bolivia still struggles against the powerful teams from Argentina and Brazil. In the 1994 games, Bolivia won just two titles, and only the tiny countries of Surinam and Aruba finished below them in the medal table. Bolivia's two gold medals came in track events. Eloy Quispe won a long distance walking race, and Policarpio Calizaya triumphed in the marathon.

Basketball is the second most popular sport, followed by volleyball, and there are nationwide league competitions for both sports.

Wealthy people are likely to try sailing or golf. La Paz has the highest golf course in the world. Because of the thin air, players find they can hit the ball longer distances than at sea level. Tennis and racketball are also popular. The latest craze with the rich Bolivians is motor sports, particularly gocarts and motorbike racing. Some of the world's toughest long distance rally races pass through Bolivia.

The Bolivian Andes offer some of the best mountain climbing in the world. The king of Bolivian mountain climbing is Bernard Guarachi. He has been to the top of Illimani more than 150 times and has traveled around the world climbing the great peaks. He is often called on to make rescue climbs and once carried an injured climber down from the mountain on his back.

SHOESHINE BOYS

Shoeshine boys are an everyday scene in Bolivian towns. They range in age from young boys of 6 or 7 to old men. Some have permanent chairs, almost like thrones, where customers climb up and have their shoes polished while they read the newspaper. Other shoeshine boys carry all their equipment with them in a small box and wait around park benches for customers.

Most middle-class Bolivians take extreme pride in their appearance and like to have smart, shining shoes. However, it does seem as if having somebody waiting on them is also part of the enjoyment.

FRIDAY NIGHT ON THE TOWN

One of the most popular leisure activities for men is the Friday night out with their friends. It is known as *viernes de soltero* ("VYAIR-nays day sohl-TAY-roh"), or single on Friday, when even married men pretend they are single for the night. Primarily this is a middle-class custom.

After work on Friday, many men do not go home at all but go straight out with co-workers to drink and play dice. Men are under considerable pressure from their peers to join such groups. Peer pressure also leads to people drinking more than is really good for them.

Many women put up with their husbands coming home drunk at two or three in the morning because the viernes de soltero is deeply ingrained in South American culture. However, the attitude toward these Friday nights out is slowly changing. One trend is for wives to go out together rather than sitting at home waiting for their husbands.

The viernes de soltero has never been part of the rural culture, although some Aymará and Quechua men have adopted it along with other aspects of the urban lifestyle.

FESTIVALS

FESTIVALS PLAY A MAJOR PART in Bolivian culture. There are ancient festivals that go back to Incan times and religious celebrations that are the legacy of centuries of Spanish rule. At fiesta time, the two cultures often become interwoven, with older Incan ceremonies being incorporated into modern religious celebrations.

Some *fiestas* ("fee-AY-stas") are celebrated throughout the country, and others are regional. Each department has its own public holiday, and most towns and villages have a festival for their special patron saint. There are also events that take place several times a year or even weekly. The Copacabana car blessing ceremony is a good example of a weekly celebration.

Fiestas are an important part of religious life and are major social occasions that bind communities together. Influential individuals who sponsor the fiestas often do so to secure their own position in society and build on their power and prestige.

Bolivians are usually happy to celebrate, whatever the occasion, and festivals quickly turn into colorful parties with street parades, dance, music, fireworks, craft sales, games, piñatas, feasting, and drinking. As another activity that forms part of the fiesta fun, young men throw water bombs—balloons filled with water—at each other and anybody else who happens to be nearby.

For most people, fiestas give an important two- or three-day break from the daily routine. Indeed, in the past, it was probably only the chewing of coca and the thought of another festival that enabled the working class population to live with their wretched conditions.

Opposite: **Auki-Auki dancers portray the Spanish conquerors at a festival.**

Above: **The queen of the Tarabuco Phujllay festival.**

Dancing at a rural festival. Fiestas in rural areas tend to be more relaxed and easygoing and are largely organized by the local community for their own entertainment. An event like El Gran Poder in La Paz attracts people from all over the country and requires months of planning and coordination with city officials, the police, and the tourist office.

EL GRAN PODER

El Gran Poder ("el grahn poh-DAIR") is a recent festival that started as a simple candlelit procession through the streets of La Paz in 1939. Since then, El Gran Poder has grown to become today's great street parade.

The parade marches for eight miles around the streets of La Paz, testing the stamina of the dancers but delighting the crowd of people, who come from all over the world. The range of costumes is magnificent and reflects every aspect of Bolivian history and mythology. The most famous dancers are *Los Morenos* ("moh-RAY-nohs"), whose costumes represent Africans.

FIESTA DEL ESPIRITU

The *Fiesta del Espiritu* is rooted in the mining traditions of Potosí. It is an occasion for the miners to make an offering to Pachamama, the earth mother, in the hope that she will protect them. The festival is staged on the last three Saturdays in June, and then again in August.

In the days leading up to the festival, villagers bring llamas into town, until the streets look like one great animal market. Each mine selects one of their workers to buy a llama for their mine. The purchases take place on the morning of the festival and are followed by an hour or so of drinking and chewing coca. At midday, the llamas are sacrificed. Some of the blood is caught and thrown down the mine, and later the stomach, feet, and head are buried as a further offering. After the sacrifice, the men return to their drinking while the women prepare the llama meat for the feast that follows.

ALACITAS FESTIVAL

Alacitas, or the festival of abundance, is an Aymará festival that takes place in La Paz and around Lake Titicaca. It is held on different dates in different towns, but in the capital, it takes place on January 24. Originally Alacitas was to ensure a good crop and was staged in September, which is the Bolivian spring. The Spanish moved the festival to January.

Ekeko with accessories. Ekeko's gifts are no longer limited to a good crop but might include money, a house, and a car. When people present Ekeko with money, they usually give him copies of U.S. dollars rather than bolivianos.

The festival centers around Ekeko, the god of the household and possessions. On the festival day, there is a whole street of stalls selling models of Ekeko and tiny accessories that people can buy for him. These represent everything people wish to receive themselves.

It is thought good luck to buy these items at exactly 12 o'clock, which means there is a terrible rush with everybody pushing and shoving. It is also luckier to have the items given to you by a friend than to buy them yourself.

COSTUMES AND MASKS

Costumes are a particularly important part of any fiesta, and a whole folk art has grown up around making costumes and masks. These change yearly, with new ideas incorporated all the time. A famous costume maker was once asked why he added dragons to the devil's mask, and he replied that he had seen them in a Chinese movie! The major parades are now televised, so a new costume that appears in La Paz might be used in Oruro a few months later. A general trend has been for the work to become more dramatic in design but less carefully made.

People not directly involved also dress up in their best clothes, and even the poorest farmer usually owns a dark European suit that is set aside for festival days. As always, native women prefer traditional dress and put on layer after layer of their most colorful skirts and their best embroidered shawls.

Los Morenos In their raised embroidery with silver threads, Los Morenos look almost like robots from a science fiction movie. With their exaggerated lips and teeth, they represent the African slaves. *Matracas* ("mah-TRAH-kahs"), a kind of rattle, are an important feature of Los Morenos' dance. The rattles come in all sorts of designs, sometimes with models of tractors, footballs, or even computers fixed onto them. Since about 1990, women have been allowed to dance alongside Los Morenos in the parade.

Auki-Auki These dancers represent old colonial men. They wear a cloak, but their main feature is the mask with its long pointed nose and an oversized top hat. This is covered with streamers that run down the back. The costume is completed by a long white beard and a twisted cane.

Devils The famous devils from the Oruro festival wear white or red body suits with gloves and boots in the same color. They have a heavily embroidered breastplate and a belt made up of hundreds of coins. Their masks are the most dramatic feature and have bulging eyes and twisted horns.

Bears Many people dress as animals, particularly bears and condors. The bear costume consist of a fur body suit, usually brown or black, often with a white chest. The mask is large and ferocious, and the teeth might be made from mirrors to catch the sunlight.

Angels The angels wear white clothing with colored tights and a pink mask. The boots and other trimming are often sky blue. They wear silver helmets and carry a small shield and a sword, making them look almost like a European knight in armor. Wings are sometimes attached to the costume.

A young dancer at the Oruro festival. New dancers promise to dance for the Virgin for three years. A four-month period of rehearsal then gets underway.

ORURO FESTIVAL

The largest carnivals are generally those staged in February and March, in the weeks leading up to Lent. All major Bolivian towns stage week-long festivals at this time, but the largest and most famous is *la Diablada*, the dance of the devil, which takes place in mining town of Oruro.

The festival is based on local folklore. Legend tells that the Virgin of Candelaria took pity on a thief who had been mortally wounded in a robbery and helped him home so he could die in his own village. The next morning, the local people found his body draped over a statue of the Virgin.

The grand parade takes part on the opening day of the festival. First come the cars and trucks decorated with jewelry, coins, and silver. Then come the dance troupes led by the Archangel Michael, dressed in sky blue and carrying his sword and shield. He is followed by people dressed as bears, condors, and devils. The devil figures wear the biggest masks of all. These are carved with horns and serpents, and sometimes even bulging flashing lights for eyes. After that there are people dressed as Incas, Kallaway medicine men, dancers with headdresses of tropical feathers, conquistadores, and miners carrying gifts for El Tío.

The parade finishes at the stadium, where the diablada takes place. *Supay* ("SOO-pay"), an evil spirit believed to live in the center of the earth, fights Saint Michael in a ritual dance, in which the forces of good triumph.

CHRISTMAS

In urban areas, Christmas is celebrated in much the same way as in the United States. Celebrations in the countryside have more to do with farming and the seasons and are really a continuation of the Incan Festival of the Sun. At this time of year, the crops have just been planted and the llamas have given birth, so everything is very vulnerable. The Aymará used to make little clay models of each of their animals at this time to bring good luck, but this tradition has been largely forgotten. Aymará people attend church on Christmas, but do not give gifts.

The *villancicos* ("vee-yan-SEE-kos") are groups of children who dress in costume or just put on a poncho and go around the streets playing drums and other instruments. It is traditional to give the villancicos small gifts of food or money.

The main Christmas decoration in the home has always been a nativity scene. From December 15 on, whole streets are lined with market stalls selling polystyrene grottos and plaster figures to place in them.

On Christmas eve, families attend midnight Mass, and then relations go back to one house together. When they arrive, in the early hours of Christmas day, they have the main Christmas meal of *picana* ("pee-CAH-nah"). This is a stew with chicken, beef, pork, vegetables, chunks of corn, potatoes, and wine or beer. Dessert is custard flan or *pandulce* ("pahn-DOOL-say"), a bread with nuts and raisins. After the meal, the family exchanges presents. Then, at two or three in the morning, they go to bed.

Stores in La Paz put on more elaborate Christmas displays each year, and men dressed as Santa Claus sometimes appear outside the shops.

OTHER HOLIDAYS

Bolivia also has several secular celebrations.

NEW YEAR'S The New Year is celebrated with one great party. Generally families gather at one house and see the new year in together. After midnight, the younger people might go to a disco while the older family members continue with the party at home.

On these occasions, the host family provides food, but it is common for everyone to pay something toward the cost. As at Christmas, picana is the main meal, but at about 6:00 in the morning, a pork soup called *fricase* ("FREE-kah-say") is served. Fricase is said to be particularly good for people who have drunk too much! After that, people drift home to sleep.

An increasingly common alternative for wealthy people is to attend an organized New Year's celebration at their sports or social club.

HISTORIC AND POLITICAL HOLIDAYS Bolivia also has several holidays that celebrate important historic and political anniversaries. Labor Day is on May 1. Most people who work in big organizations gather for meetings and speeches, and there are organized marches.

Discovery of America Day is on October 12. This used to be a holiday, but the 500th anniversary celebration became a controversial issue in Bolivia. Indigenous Bolivians protested that their ancestors had been in America for hundreds of years before Columbus arrived. The government abandoned the holiday.

National Day, on August 6, is celebrated with a parade.

FESTIVALS CALENDAR

January
Kings Day. Celebrates the day the three wise men visited baby Jesus.

Alacitas Fair. Festival dedicated to Ekeko. The main celebration is in La Paz.

February
Fiesta of the Virgin of Candelaria. Celebrated in several towns, although the main event is in Copacabana.

La Diablada Carnival. Great street parade followed by devils' dance in Oruro. The largest and most famous of a nationwide series of pre-Lent carnivals.

March
Fiesta de la Uva. A grape festival in Tarija.

Phujllay. A very dramatic festival staged in Tarabuco, near Sucre. Dancers and musicians celebrate the Battle of Lumbati.

March-April
Easter. Takes place throughout the country.

May
Festival of the Cross. Celebrations in various Bolivian towns, most notably in Tarija, where the festival lasts nearly two weeks.

Mothers' Day. A nationwide celebration, but particularly important in Cochabamba, where the women of the town once defended the city from Spanish troops.

June
Festival of the Holy Trinity. Takes place in the city of Trinidad. Bullfighting is featured.

San Juan Midyear Festival. Staged at the height of the cold months. People light fires on the hillside or in the doorway of their houses and leap over the fires to bring good luck. The fires also represent the warmer months that lie ahead.

July
Fiesta del Santo Patrono de Moxos. **A** major festival in the village of San Ignacio de Moxos. The festival is famous for its wild dancing.

August
National Day. Celebrations take place throughout the country on August 6.

Festival of the Virgin of Urcupiña. Staged in the town of Quillacollo, this is the largest festival in Cochabamba department.

September
Festival of San Roque. Mainly a Tarija event in honor of Saint Roque. He was the patron saint of dogs, and this is reflected in the costumes.

October
Festival of the Virgin of Rosario. Festivals take place in many Bolivian towns.

November
All Saints' Day. On November 1 and 2, Bolivians visit the graves of their relations.

December
Christmas. Celebrated throughout Bolivia.

FOOD

MEALS IN BOLIVIA ARE BASED ON a great many recipes for a few staple foods. There is considerable regional variety, but wherever you are, meat is likely to form the central part of the diet and is usually served with rice or potatoes and sometimes both.

Bread also plays a large part in the Bolivian diet. Bolivia grows wheat around Santa Cruz and also receives grain from the United States. There are bread sellers on every street corner, and the price is subsidized by the government.

Diet is influenced by the region people live in and their income. Potatoes are the staple food in the highlands, but in the lowlands they are largely replaced by rice, plantain, and yucca. A family in the Altiplano generally has less access to vegetables and fruit than a family living in the lowlands. Middle-class families have far greater variety in their diet.

The style and taste of bread varies from city to city, but in La Paz miniature French loaves are the most popular. A dozen of these loaves cost around 50 cents.

Opposite: **The witches' market in La Paz sells a variety of herbs.**

Left: **A street stall offers a wide range of snacks.**

Selling potatoes at the market in Cochabamba. There are many different kinds of potatoes in the Andes, including yellow and purple varieties.

Llama meat is seldom eaten by middle-class people, who consider it inferior to beef. However, llama meat is lower in fat and might well be healthier than beef.

POTATOES AND OTHER TUBERS

Even allowing for regional variations, potatoes and other tuberous plants make up a major part of the Bolivian diet. Potatoes come in various sizes and colors, with claims of two or three hundred different varieties.

Potatoes originated in the Americas and were being eaten by the indigenous people there long before the Spanish arrived. The early conquistadores brought potatoes back to Spain and from there their popularity spread throughout northern Europe and Ireland.

In addition to potatoes, people eat a large number of other kinds of tuberous plants, including oca and anu. Oca are a fleshy root that grows between two and four inches long. They look like a pink sausage and can be boiled, roasted, or fried. Anu is a yellow-white plant that looks and tastes similar to a parsnip. Two other basic foods that are widely eaten are *choclo* ("CHOH-kloh"), which is a large type of corn, and habas beans. Habas beans are collected from the wild and either roasted or put in stews.

FREEZE-DRIED POTATOES

The Altiplano natives have their own way of freeze-drying potatoes and oca so that they turn into *chuño* ("CHOO-nyoh"). Any surplus crop is spread on the ground to freeze at night and then allowed to thaw in the sunlight. For several days in a row, the vegetables are trampled with bare feet to squeeze out the moisture. This finally leaves a light, dry husk that can be stored for months. Chuño can be added to stews and soups, and travelers take it on journeys because it cooks quickly.

THE MEAL PATTERN

Breakfast is called *desayuno* ("day-sie-OO-noh") and is quite simple, frequently little more than a roll with coffee. People rushing to work might stop to buy a bowl of chicken soup from a street vendor. It is not unusual to see a group of businessmen eating breakfast on a street corner.

Lunch, or *almuerzo* ("al-MWER-zoh"), is the most important meal of the day. Many restaurants offer a set lunch, including an appetizer, soup, a beef or chicken dish, and dessert. These are very popular and cost as little as 90 cents. Lunch is a leisurely occasion, even on work days, and it is not unusual to see businessmen linger over coffee in no apparent rush to get back to work. On weekends, lunch with family and friends becomes a major social event and can go on and on. Tea is served at the table, and then people resume the conversation in the garden. This is known as *sobremesa* ("soh-bray-MAY-sah"), or the after lunch hour. Frequently a guest invited for lunch is still there when the evening meal is served.

In rural areas, the meal pattern is very different. Altiplano farmers have only two meals a day, the first eaten early in the morning, the second in the evening after work. The diet in these communities is monotonous, with the basic meal made up of quinoa, oca, and potatoes. Native families usually eat outside if it is not raining. The men particularly do not feel comfortable eating openly in front of strangers, so when they are away from home, they usually face a wall when they are eating and sit hunched over their food.

Quinoa is a local grain that is high in protein. It can be ground into flour or used to thicken porridge dishes and stews.

In the countryside, cooking is either done indoors, using a large metal pot suspended over the fire, or outdoors on small clay stoves fueled with reeds or whatever else is available locally.

FAVORITE RECIPES

Most Bolivian recipes have meat in them, and beef, chicken, and fish are popular with people who can afford them. Poorer people generally have to be content with mutton, goat, or llama meat.

One of the most common dinners is *silpancho* ("seel-PAN-choh"), which is pounded beef with a egg cooked on top. Soups, stews, and broth are very popular in Bolivia. Lamb is often served this way in meals such as *thimpu* ("TEEM-poo"), which is a spicy stew cooked with vegetables. *Saice* ("SIE-say") is another meaty broth, and *fricase* is a pork soup seasoned with yellow *ají* ("ah-HEE"), or hot pepper.

Hot, spicy sauces are a popular addition to any dish. These might be made from tomatoes or pepper pods and are usually placed on the table in a small dish so that people can add as much or as little as they wish.

The lowlands diet includes many wild animals, particularly armadillo.

HUMINTAS

16 oz. (.45 kg) yellow corn
8 oz. (.23 kg) corn muffin mix prepared according to directions on package
2-3 tablespoons sugar
$1/4$ tablespoon anise seed
2 tablespoons vegetable oil
$1/4$ tablespoon cinnamon
1 $1/2$ cups grated white cheese
$1/4$ tablespoon ground red pepper

Put the cheese and red pepper to one side. Mix all the other ingredients in a food processor until they are well mixed and the corn is coarsely ground. Pour the mixture into a greased pan. Sprinkle cheese and red pepper on top. Bake in oven at 400° for 25 minutes or until done.

FRUITS AND DESSERTS

Bolivia has an excellent selection of fruits. These include several fruits that are not easily available in the United States, such as custard apples, prickly pear cactus, passion fruits, and a whole range of mangos.

Desserts with a local flavor include *tojori* ("toh-HOH-ree") and *thaya* ("TIE-ah"). Tojori are made from corn, cinnamon, and sugar all mashed together. Thaya are a favorite on the Altiplano and are made from apple puree mixed with sugared water and spiced with cinnamon and cloves. This mixture is shaped into little domes and placed on the roof of the house to freeze overnight. In the morning, a little sugar water colored with local spices is added. The town of Potosí specializes in pastries, including *tawa-tawas*, which are deep-fried pastries served in syrup.

A special dessert saved for festivals are *confites* ("kohn-FEE-tays"), which are made by the local confectioner and sold on festival days. They are made from boiled sugar syrup hardened around nuts, aniseed, fruit, biscuits, or coconuts, and they come in an amazing variety of colors.

Bolivia has many varieties of bananas, some of which are used for cooking. Bananas baked in their skins are a favorite desert or snack.

EXCELLENT CHEESES

Bolivia has a wide range of cheeses, many of which are excellent. In the Altiplano, cheese made out of sheep's milk is the most common. It is slightly soft cheese, almost like a French brie, but it does have a rather strong smell that some people dislike. Certainly middle-class Bolivians seem to prefer the more expensive cheeses made from cow's milk. The best Bolivian cheeses are generally thought to be those from Tarija department.

Milk is sold in Bolivian shops, but it can be hard to find in the smaller towns. Sometimes milk is sold fresh from the farm without being pasteurized or treated in any way, which can spread disease.

Salteñas for sale from a street vendor.

STREET FOOD

In the cities, the favorite snack is the *salteña* ("sal-TAY-nyah"). These oval pies are eaten as a quick lunch or a tasty and filling snack. Salteñas are stuffed with chicken or beef and whatever else is available. This might include different vegetables, eggs, potatoes, and onions. The final touch is a big helping of spices to give them their distinctive taste. Salteñas are the subject of considerable debate, and everyone seems to know one shop or stall that bakes the very best in town.

Empanadas ("em-pah-NAH-dahs") are filled with either beef, chicken, or cheese. They can be baked in bread or deep fried in fat. Another fast food specialty is *humintas* ("oo-MEEN-tahs"). These are made from cornmeal with various additional fillings, shaped into a triangle, and wrapped in a corn husk. Like salteñas, they come in many different varieties.

Bolivia's traditional fast foods are coming under considerable competition from hamburgers and french fries. In big cities, these are sold from little kiosks on every street and are extremely popular.

DRINKS

Black tea is probably the most common Bolivian drink. It is served strong, with lots of sugar. *Mate de coca* ("MAH-tay day KOH-kah"), which is tea with coca leaves added, is also very popular and is said to be a good cure for altitude sickness.

Refresco ("ray-FRES-koh") is a fruit juice with a dried peach in the bottom of the glass. *Tostada* is made from a combination of barley, honey, cinnamon, and cloves. These are mixed in plastic containers and poured into glasses waiting for thirsty

Men drinking chicha in a Cochabamba chicha house.

customers. A metal saucer is placed on top to keep the dirt and dust out, but when one person has finished drinking, the glass is often just given a quick wipe with a cloth before being filled up ready for the next person.

Chicha is a potent, homemade corn beer that has been brewed since Incan times and probably for hundreds of years before then. To make chicha, women chew corn into small balls called *muko* ("MOO-koh") and leave these to dry in the sun. The muko are then boiled with chunks of meat, grain, and sugar. Spices give a regional flavor to each brew. Local people know which houses chicha is brewed in, and on festival days people walk around the streets selling it by the glass.

There is also a drink called *singani* ("seen-GAH-nee") that is made from grapes and is a cross between whiskey and wine. In addition, modern breweries offer a selection of excellent beers.

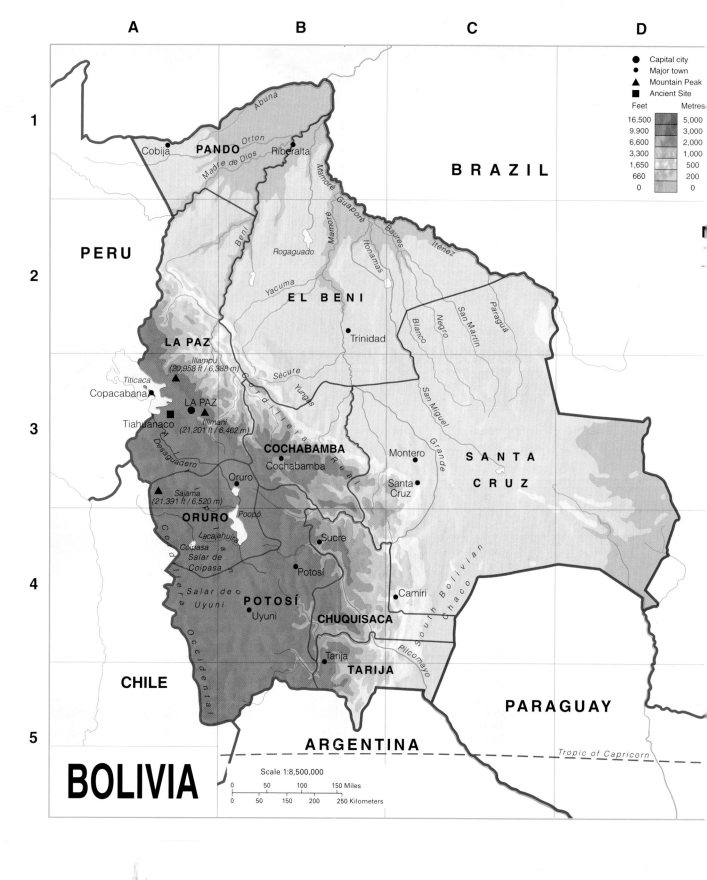

A   **B**   **C**   **D**

● Capital city
• Major town
▲ Mountain Peak
■ Ancient Site

Feet		Metres
16,500		5,000
9,900		3,000
6,600		2,000
3,300		1,000
1,650		500
660		200
0		0

1

Cobija

Abuná

PANDO

Orton

Riberalta

Madre de Dios

B R A Z I L

Mamoré Guaporé

Beni

Rogaguado

Baures

Itenez

PERU

2

Yacuma

E L   B E N I

Paraguá

Itonamas

Trinidad

Blanco

Negro

San Martín

LA PAZ

*Illampu
(20,958 ft / 6,388 m)* ▲

Titicaca

Sécure

Copacabana ▲

■   LA PAZ ●

Yungas

▲ *Illimani
(21,201 ft / 6,462 m)*

Montero

S A N T A

3

Tiahuanaco

Desaguadero

Cordillera Real

COCHABAMBA

Cochabamba

Santa
Cruz

C R U Z

San Miguel

▲ *Sajama
(21,391 ft / 6,520 m)*

Oruro

Poopó

ORURO

Lacajahuira

Grande

Coipasa

*Salar de
Coipasa*

Sucre

4

*Salar de
Uyuni*

POTOSÍ

Uyuni

Potosí

Camiri

South Bolivian Chaco

Cordillera Occidental

CHUQUISACA

CHILE

Tarija

Pilcomayo

TARIJA

PARAGUAY

5

ARGENTINA

Tropic of Capricorn

BOLIVIA

Scale 1:8,500,000

0   50   100   150 Miles

0   50   150   200   250 Kilometers

QUICK NOTES

AREA
424,165 sq mi (1,098,581 sq km)

POPULATION
7,832,000 (1992)

MAIN GROUPS
Native, 60%; Mestizo, 30%; Spanish, 10%
(statistics on racial groups vary considerably)

MAJOR RELIGION
Roman Catholic: 95%

PRESIDENT
Gonzalo Sánchez de Lozada (1993)

MAJOR INDUSTRIES
Textiles, food processing, mining

MAJOR CROPS
Potatoes, sugar, coffee, corn, rubber

NATURAL RESOURCES
Antimony, tin, tungsten, silver, zinc, iron, silver, gold, gas, oil

LIFE EXPECTANCY
59 men, 64 women

CAPITAL
La Paz

DEPARTMENTS
El Beni, Chuquisaca, Cochabamba, La Paz, Oruro, Pando, Potosi, Santa Cruz, Tarija

MAJOR CITIES

La Paz	1,049,000
Santa Cruz	615,000
Cochabamba	377,000
Oruro	195,000
Potosí	114,000
Sucre	95,000

MAJOR LAKES
Lake Titicaca, Lake Poopó

MAJOR RIVERS
Beni, Mamoré, Desaguadero, Pilcomayo, Paraguay, Plate

HIGHEST POINT
Sajama (21,391 ft/6,519 m)

OFFICIAL LANGUAGES
Spanish, Quechua, Aymará

LEADERS IN POLITICS
Gonzalo Sánchez de Lozada: president elected 1993
Luis García Meza: military dictator, seized power 1980
General Hugo Bánzer Suárez: military dictator, seized power 1971, ruled until 1978; subsequently a candidate in elections of 1985 and 1989
Victor Paz Estenssoro: leader of the 1952 revolution, effected extensive social, political, and economic reforms

CURRENCY
Boliviano (4.77 bolivianos = US$1)

GLOSSARY

Altiplano ("ahl-tee-PLAH-noh")
Also known as the High Plateau, a large expanse of high, flat land between two ranges of the Andes.

amautu ("ah-MOW-too")
Wise men who traditonally memorized vast amounts of information.

ayni ("AYE-nee")
A social system in which men of the village make decisions communally.

bombin ("bohm-BEEN")
Bolivian name for a bowler hat, frequently worn by native highland women.

campesino ("kam-pay-SEE-noh")
A peasant or small scale farmer. Since 1952, the official term for native peoples.

cha'lla ("CHAY-ya")
A ritual blessing, frequently drawn from a combination of Christian and native beliefs.

chulla ("CHOO-lah")
A knit hat with ear flaps worn by native highland men.

chuño ("CHOO-nyoh")
Potatoes that have been frozen and then dried in the sun.

cucho ("KOO-choh")
A ritual offering placed in the foundation of a new building.

mantu ("MAHN-too")
Shawl worn by native highland women that can be folded to carry babies or other loads.

mestizo
Person of mixed native and European ancestry.

padrino ("pah-DREE-noh")
Godparent.

quenas ("KAY-nas")
Flutes made from reed pipes.

salteñas ("sal-TAY-nyahs")
Spicy meat pies often eaten as a snack.

sobremesa ("soh-bray-MAY-sah")
The after-lunch hour, when people talk.

soroche ("so-ROH-shay")
Altitude sickness, a frequent problem in La Paz.

surazo ("soo-RAH-zoh")
Cold winds that blow in from the Argentine pampas.

El Tío ("TEE-oh")
Literally "uncle," the name for the native god of minerals, patron of miners.

viernes de soltero
("VYAIR-nays day sol-TAY-roh")
Literally "single on Friday," the Hispanic custom for men to go out without their wives on Friday nights to drink and play dice.

BIBLIOGRAPHY

Blair, David N. *The Land and People of Bolivia*. New York: J.B. Lippincott, 1990.

Hudson, Rex A. and Dennis M. Hanratty, eds. *Bolivia: A Country Study*. Washington, D.C.: U.S. Government Printing Office, 1991.

Klein, Herbert S. *Bolivia: the Evolution of a Multi-Ethnic Society*, 2nd Edition. New York: Oxford University Press, 1992.

Morales, Waltrand Q. *Bolivia: Land of Struggle*. Boulder, Colorado: Westview Press, 1992.

INDEX

INDEX

INDEX